MOM, THERE'S A SCORPION IN MY PANTS

One Family's Year of Living Purposefully in Rural Nicaragua

Cully Lundgren

Book designed by Carl Peterson
xsldesigns.com

Set in Garamond Typeface

Printed by CreateSpace, An Amazon.com Company

Dedicated to the ones I love - Miriam, Harlan, and Olle, who were willing to risk so much.

Thank you guys. You continue to teach me what it means to be vulnerable and brave.

Many of the people who need to be thanked for this book will likely never even know they are featured in the following pages. These are the people of El Tololar, who continue to live their seemingly unremarkable lives in remarkable ways. Muchas Gracias to all of you, for welcoming us in. You are in our thoughts and prayers every day. Thanks go to Tyler St. Clare, Executive Director of Tololamos. Tyler, we never knew where that first piano lesson would lead.

Thanks go to all of our friends and family who supported our trip. Special thanks go to Harlan and Faye Muntz, who not only supported us financially (and helped get the book's author to overcome his inertia and bring it to the finish line) but also visited our family at a crucial time. Special thanks also to the Arshad-Powell Clan, the only visitors who stayed with us in El Tololar, getting a real taste of what life was like. Kelley and Imran, thanks also for your critical eyes on various versions of this book. Thanks Anthonys so much for the two weeks of amazing and restful time we spent together. Thanks Jen, Chris and Mardi for joining that adventure. Thanks also to the Davises, for taking a chance on Nicaragua for your family vacation. Thank you Larry for your bravery in coming here to Boston and continuing our cross-cultural connection.

Helen, your painting (the cover of this book) is perfect. How you captured the feel and texture of our Nicaraguan home from a photo is beyond me. Thank you! Big props to Carl Peterson, for formatting the text and the cover, and helping me figure out what needed to be done to finalize the self-publishing process.

Thank you Nicaragua, for providing the welcoming context of people and place in which we lived, and loved, and wrote.

CONTENTS

Foreword

What if you and your family had the chance to do something audacious? Something crazy, earth shattering, so transcendent it was out of the realm of what your city-living, soccer-kid toting, traffic-enduring head could imagine. What if you could muster up your collective courage and leap into the unknown, strongly sensing but never being sure that your great leap would someday pay off. What if?? Recently, one family – perhaps one not so different from yours – took one such leap, a leap that landed them, of all places, in a tiny village in Nicaragua. A place where running water was a rarity and most of the population lived in poverty. A place where scorpions were in your bed sheets, cockroaches were kings of the latrines, and rice and beans were often all there was to eat. A place where hearts were huge, generosity was everywhere, and welcoming strangers was a way of life. Into this unknown jumped one family, beginning a year-long odyssey they would never forget.

It's hard to say exactly where or when the idea was born but certainly Cully, having spent most of his career working in the international development realm, had always wanted to impart to his children a unique experience of living abroad. His wife Miriam, a Midwest born dancer and Pilates instructor was happy living in Boston, making a difference with her art and her clients, one soul, one body at a time; moving to another country was not her thing. Their two sons Harlan (11) and Olle (9) liked their school, friends and sports and couldn't really get their heads around what living elsewhere meant. And where was Nicaragua anyway?

In 2015 it began to come together, thanks to the dream of Harlan's former piano teacher, the profound faith and strength of

Miriam, and two young boys who displayed courage beyond their years. So the Lundgren family jumped – actually it was more of a plunge – into the unknown. They began to share their idea with family and friends and it resonated with many at a core level. The typical response went something like this: "That is amazing; what a great thing to do. But our family could never do that. We are just too busy with life here; we couldn't risk it. But we want to support and follow you, because this is something extraordinary."

Equipped with the financial and emotional backing of an army of generous, amazing people, the Lundgrens quit their jobs, sold their car, rented their house and did the thousand other things required to detach them from life in the States. They collaborated with Tyler St. Clare, a former Peace Corps Volunteer in Nicaragua. Working with Tyler, the Lundgrens raised the money to build their house, one that would be gifted to another family when they left. On September 1st, 2016, they arrived in El Tololar, trembling with both fear and excitement, not knowing Spanish, and wondering what they had actually got themselves into. They were met that first night, under the freshly thatched-roof patio of their house, by the extended Rivas family, their hosts for the next year. Little did they know that each one of these strangers would soon come to be their family.

Over the course of the next year, the Lundgrens experienced an almost unprecedented range of physical and emotional challenges. Their eleven-year-old son Harlan, sorely missing his friends and first year of middle school back home, became the poster child for injuries and disorders such as warts, diarrhea, cuts, scrapes, fevers, rashes, and nausea. You name it, he got it, and yet he persevered, waking up and greeting each day with a dogged tenacity that said, "I can do this." Nine-year-old Olle endured his share of ailments, and had profound moments of missing life and friends back home but he persisted, finding the beauty and the goodness in the otherwise mundane, using his imagination to lift spirits. Miriam, always having possessed a deep faith in God and people, used trust and grace to dance, or at times plow, through a daily parade of obstacles and challenges. Cully, living out his lifelong dream, made the most of every minute and tried to balance the difficulties his family faced with the adventure that stood before them.

They took it step by step, one plate of rice and beans at a time. They started to learn Spanish, teach English, and make friends with their new neighbors. They volunteered their time with Tololamos – the local non-profit Tyler had started – to help identify needs in the community. Using the funds they had raised from friends and family back home, they provided scholarships to two university students and five high school students. They provided resources to the local health clinic, and helped Tololamos plant 6,000 trees as part of their tree nursery project.

They also explored other ways they could help the local people they met, in small but often meaningful ways. Their "people investments" ranged from buying a horse for their friend Ivania so that she could pull her cart to the local elementary school and sell her delicious snacks, to investing in several local small businesses, to providing a much-needed down payment for a motorcycle for their neighbors. They learned that a little bit can go a long way, and that a small sacrifice on their part could be life-changing for the people of El Tololar. The horse they helped buy, for instance, cost the same as a one night's stay at an inexpensive hotel in New York City. Their investments were meant to be holistic, addressing not only a family's economic needs, but their social, physical and emotional ones as well. Yet herein lay the irony, as it became their own needs, fears and insecurities that were consistently met with love and grace by their Nicaraguan neighbors.

Over the course of the year they experienced earthquakes, scorpion stings, tarantula scares, biting ants at every turn, air infused with gnats and flies, frequent lack of water and electricity, intense heat and dust, despair, profound sadness, known and unknown diseases, and a sense of loneliness. At the same time, they felt love and connection. They persevered, and began to experience the power of community. They learned how to see and have grace for others (including themselves), and that people have more in common than we think, as long as we are willing to see beyond and through the stereotypes we have created of others.

At times, life was an all-out toil. It was hard to see the positive, for example, when you are frequently forced to spend much of the night sweeping waves of water out of your bedrooms during the rainy season. It can be equally hard to be upbeat when the dust from the nearby fallow peanut fields becomes so thick that you can't even eat or drink, or see your kids, without getting dirt in your eyes, mouth and nose. And going without water on a regular basis – a rare phenomenon back home – was just plain depressing. At other times, their updates to family and friends back home seemed implausible. "Your cat really got stung by a giant scorpion and died?" People would ask. "Miriam had a tarantula crawl up her arm while doing laundry, say it isn't so." "Harlan and Olle really had to walk 45 minutes to school, on dusty, cow-poop filled paths?" The stories became part of the fabric of their daily lives, a type of badge that said they had lived through another day, they had overcome.

But in the midst of the daily grind, they experienced life in Nicaragua in a way they never could have by just traveling through. Their neighbors were not just the people they waved at from afar when they returned from work; they became brothers and sisters, mothers and fathers. For almost a year, the Lundgrens were given a unique insight into another culture, learning the rhythms, the sights and the sounds of daily life. Corn, for example, became much more than a vegetable they bought at the supermarket. It was the lifeblood of people around them, and learning the ways in which it was planted, grown, harvested, and turned into myriad types of food was a deep experience unto itself.

As their odyssey came to an end, the Lundgrens realized that perhaps their cross-cultural experience could be of value to others, especially families with children, in four specific ways.

First, at a time when the political climate in the United States has polarized institutional and personal relationships like never before – often exposing differences rather than highlighting commonalities – possibly their experience of living with "the other" could help reveal a different way to educate our children concerning our neighbor, or colleague, and especially about those that think differently than we do. Maybe, just maybe, we will find that we have more in common with those who think differently than we want to believe.

Second, as the North American culture of connecting, uploading and plugging in continues to pervade our every waking hour, a glimpse inside a different way of living, more simply, more connected to each other and the earth, could also be of use. Perhaps we can hit the pause button on the desire to consume more information and more things. Amidst the clutter and noise of life, maybe there is another way to live.

Third, perhaps one of the big concerns holding us back from pursuing our own dreams is a fear of losing our own perceived security. Is it possible that we have huge dreams that go unfulfilled because it is just too scary or too much work to take that first step?

Finally, we learned that no matter how hard you try, you will ultimately only be successful in life when operating in community, and we all have communities that are integral to our lives, no matter where we live.

After reading this book that details the Lundgren's year in Nicaragua in raw, sometimes gory detail, readers might ask themselves four simple questions: How can I reach out to "the others" in my life? What dreams am I ignoring? What is holding me back? Who can I ask to join me on my journey?

Chapter 1:
Touchdown

Late August

Dear Great Friends and Loved Ones,

After many moons of preparations and a crazy family road trip across the US, we arrived last night in Managua, Nicaragua! We are all in great spirits and ready for this adventure to finally begin. Tomorrow, our good friend Tyler St. Clare will meet us here in the capital city of Managua and we will drive (with our belongings enclosed in seven, 50lb bags) to the village of El Tololar, our home for the next year. We will spend the following days setting up our home with our new friends from the village.

By next week, we will be settled in, hopefully having learned some Spanish, at least a little more. As this is our first update, we'll keep it short and sweet. Future ones will include pictures and more "Nica" flavor.

Many, many thanks to all of you for your support, prayers, and encouragement en route. We feel so loved and that you are with us on this journey.

Hasta Luego and we will be in touch again soon.

Chapter 2:
The Village People

Early September, 2016

Our first experience in Nicaragua came from the rather posh Camino Real Hotel near the airport in Managua; there was a nice, clean pool, delicious food (including hamburgers!), AC, comfy beds with quilts… you name it. It was luxurious. We spent half a day seeing Managua, zip-lining upside-down over a lake and touring the central plaza where the clock over the colonial church still reads 12:29, the time at which a massive earthquake struck the country in December of 1972, killing more than 6,000 people.

After two days in Managua, our friend and Executive Director of Tololamos, Tyler St. Clare, met us at our hotel along with two good friends, Beto and Wilmar, and we were quickly ushered into our new life. We took a two-hour mini-bus ride from Managua, passing smoking volcanoes and lush green countryside. We understood almost nothing yet thanks to their generosity of spirit, managed to engage in several conversations with our travel hosts. The first part of the trip went quickly. Nicaragua had invested little in economic development except for in highway infrastructure, which was stellar. Before long we had turned right, onto the four-mile-long dirt road that led to our house.

Soon after we settled into our new *casita* (small house) in the village of El Tololar, about 45 minutes by chicken-bus from the colonial city of León. Chicken-buses are beautifully adorned yet very rustic former US school buses, found literally on every road and path across Central America. We had a new pet *gatita* (female kitten in Spanish) whom Olle named Sweetie, subsequently *Dulce (*sweet in Spanish). Harlan and Olle were making new friends, and everyone we had met was amazingly kind and gracious.

Making a final left turn onto a narrow, dusty lane, we were greeted by a slew of smiling faces, each offering to carry our bags down the winding path toward our house. Rounding a corner, there she was: two bedrooms, a large, empty kitchen, and a spacious, airy patio with a thatch roof that proved both largely waterproof and the likely abode of several small tarantulas. Harlan and Olle's room came replete with two *tijera* (scissor) beds, named for the neat way they folded up, constructed with thick shopping bag material. After introductions to what seemed like 30 different family members of the Rivas family – it actually was 30 different members of the Rivas family, including the Patriarch Don Leonel – we were treated to a small feast of rice, beans, and *Pio Quinto*, Nicaraguan rum cake. Dinner was promptly followed by dancing, mostly by Miriam and the woman who owned the property our house was built on who, coincidentally, was also named Miriam. Somehow, in the midst of so much unfamiliarity and apprehension, our differences were already being softened by something as commonplace as a name: Miriam.

Day 1 in the village dawned with the roosters, as did every day after throughout our time in El Tololar. We were surrounded by volcanoes wherever we went: San Cristobal, Telica, Santa Clara, Momotombo and of course Cerro Negro, one of the youngest volcanoes in the world and one we hoped to "surf" in the coming weeks. Our friend and staff member of Tololamos, Beto, helped electrify our kitchen. As he worked, we saw our first scorpion: just a baby. Beto worked some local magic and somehow 'decommissioned' the scorpion's ability to strike with his tail, lovingly placing the now powerless little guy in a nearby banana tree. For the record, within days we encountered two other scorpions – one in the shower and the other Miriam found early one morning (before her coffee no less!) in an oven mitt. Neither met such a nice fate as the banana scorpion.

Days 2-10 were spent getting acquainted with our new home and neighbors. We painted our house a beautiful sunny yellow shade that really made it feel homier. We dug a hole in our backyard for garbage, as that was how you had to roll in El Tololar; there was no garbage truck that came every week. We encountered hundreds and thousands of *hormigas* (biting ants). Harlan and Olle took part in a local baseball game, which included Harlan covering second, a horse in right and a couple of pigs playing center.

Each day brought new challenges and experiences. We were always sweating, and when the power went, sometimes you couldn't take a shower (the water was pump fed). A few days without a proper cleansing could make you feel like a giant walking, grimy, moist towelette. We missed all of our friends and family terribly, and it was tough to get used to the beds, although the boys actually were doing a great job adjusting to sleeping with mosquito nets, lizards, and round the clock noises of every ilk. We were under the erroneous assumption, for example, that fowl started their clatter at daybreak but it turned out *Nica* roosters cock-a doodle-doo anytime that felt right.

Miriam was learning the local way to cook *frijoles* and they were damn good. You did have to plan ahead, though, as prep and cook time take like 2½ hours. We had rainstorms most evenings and one storm was so strong that we spent several hours "sweeping" water off our patio and out of our rooms. The boys walked to the *venta* almost daily, basically a house with a small, attached store that sold soda, chips, eggs, hammocks and in a pinch, mouse and fly traps. Miriam hoed a garden plot beside our house and grew seedlings to plant carrots, beans, tomatoes, cilantro, peppers, swiss chard and squash. Getting the garden plot up and running with the proper nutrients was not easy. The process included a hilarious conversation we had in very halting Spanish with a local boy named Josue about borrowing a wheelbarrow and making a "poop" run to his house; we had been tipped off that he had some good, quality cow manure, free for the taking.

The heat, missing our loved ones, and not being able to communicate effectively represented a sampling of the daily hardships. Harlan was really sick for three days with a stomach bug last week, really the sickest we'd ever seen him. He got a gold star for pushing through such a nasty illness in the midst of all the other challenges, including the two small tarantulas (both fortunately dead) we found sprawled on our patio on successive mornings.

Tyler introduced us to many of the friends he made during his two years here as a Peace Corps volunteer, and one family offered to give us a rabbit. Olle was particularly psyched at the prospect of a kitten and a baby rabbit. We took Spanish lessons every Monday to Thursday. We hoped to improve day by day.

Our house was well built yet it still had trouble withstanding the earth-shaking, ear-splitting thunderstorms that rolled through El Tololar on many a evening, often leaving our typically dry bedroom – and especially our mattress – sopping wet. We also found out that the soil in El Tololar was loaded with iron from all the volcanic eruptions over the years, making lightning and thunder positively dazzling and utterly frightening. "Shabam! What on earth was that deafening, brilliant racket?" we said to each other on particularly stormy nights. Who knew that iron, an important but seemingly harmless dietary mineral, could produce such electrifying results in the night sky.

We encountered many funny wording here in Nicaragua, like the advertisement for the best "Polish-Sri Lankan Food" in León or the poster at the Post Office that featured a big "152nd" anniversary celebration, always a popular one! Equally funny was the boy on the local bus who wore a baseball shirt, #8, featuring the ever popular team name "Stanky Leg."

Chapter 3:
Earthquakes, Rice and Beans

Mid/Late September

Gnats love mornings, and apparently afternoons. Thankfully they don't like evenings, or at least not yet. This is just one of the lessons we are learning in Nicaragua.

Another one is that doing laundry in a Nicaraguan village is a decidedly different task than back home. Take a typical Saturday morning. We usually sleep in a bit, until about 6am when the roosters have reached fever pitch. We wake up and make coffee (what a delicious treat), accompanied by scrambled eggs, bread and succulent, local fruit. Then, the next four hours are spent doing laundry (Miriam is thus far our principal launderer). The process involves washing each piece of clothing individually with a large bar of special laundry soap. You rub the soap into the clothing, which lies on our very own cement washboard surface. Rinsing, grinding and wringing out each piece individually, you finally hang each article in the sun on the nearby barbed-wire fence. This process, while laborious, works adequately for the most part. But, during the rainy season, you need to capture the fine balance of giving the clothes maximum time in the sun while being prepared at a moment's notice to grab them off the fence as soon as the first drops of afternoon rain start falling.

Washing laundry the local way also helps you realize why the old man on the bus wears a beat up shirt with the telltale holes in the corners. Two and a half weeks of drying on barbed-wire, our clothes are still intact, with surprisingly few tears.

One night not long after we arrived, we awoke to a violent shaking of the house. Miriam quickly ascertained it was an earthquake, and our friend Tyler (it was his last night in El Tololar before returning to Baltimore) was at our door not long after, requesting that we exit our rooms for a few minutes per quake protocol. It took us a minute to wake up Harlan and Olle, who had slept right through the 5.8 magnitude tremor. Our neighbors (we are surrounded on all sides by various members of the Rivas family) had the TV on and let us know that the epicenter was near *Momotombo*, a very active volcano to our south. No eruptions or increased activity were reported, so we were free to go back to bed. There were multiple follow-up tremors the rest of the night, and further sleep proved elusive.

Saturday and Sunday afternoons are often about baseball and soccer. The baseball games are all about the kids, and Harlan and Olle join in when they can. The local boys are excellent, natural ball players, and seem to play all the time. Big Papi and the Red Sox are very well known here, and we inevitably get fist-bumps when we sport our Sox apparel.

Soccer games are played in Don Leonel's front yard. He is the 77 year-old patriarch of the family. His yard has a rich, organic, volcanic dirt surface and is just the right size for a four or five on five game, with only a few giant banana plants, one huge grapefruit tree, some roots and rocks, and a deep water well as obstacles. We tried playing barefoot but quickly realized our feet are supremely soft. Most of our local friends play barefoot or in flip flops – which seems even harder – and there are a few players who could no doubt thrive at the collegiate or even professional level. Soccer is a great way to learn and use Spanish as well, and our hosts are always gracious with our fumbling skills in both areas, even when we clumsily step on their shoeless toes with our heavy sneakers.

Across the road from the soccer patch lies one of many fields of peanuts where we run at dusk most evenings. It is one of the true pleasures of life, to run barefoot through a verdantly green field of peanuts, the field framed by at least four or five volcanoes, our runs punctuated by almost nightly lightning storms.

Getting a reliable Internet connection at our house has been a challenge, so most weekdays revolve around finding good Wi-Fi access for the boys' schooling. We take the 7am chicken bus to León – chickens do ride the bus, but infrequently– and arrive at the final stop just after 8am. We then either walk, take a taxi, or a 3-wheeled bicycle to one of several cafes advertising Wi-Fi; if we are lucky, it actually works. Miriam and the boys do school work till noon, and Cully usually goes grocery shopping during that time. We try to buy rice, beans, fruits and vegetables at the local market near the bus terminal, where we can generally get them for a better rate than at the international stores. We fundraised for the year and try to stick to a budget of $130-$150 a week. Shopping exclusively at the Walmart-owned *La Union* grocery store near León's beautiful cathedral would quickly put us over our budget. Plus, bargaining is fun, as is getting to know the banana man, the cabbage girl, the pineapple dude and the watermelon lady.

It isn't easy for the boys to concentrate while holding class in a restaurant. Inevitably several times during the day a beat-up truck will drive by with a megaphone, blaring out advertisements for anything from green plantains to an upcoming dance party. At one coffee house, a woman came in begging for money during math class for Harlan and language arts for Olle. The boys are beginning to gain a good understanding about how to accept the challenges, and at the same time make space to mourn the fact that they miss their friends, family and life back at home. They push through each day, and while classes at times end in yelling, stomping, or vacating the premises in anger over a particularly difficult assignment, they persevere.

After school we walk or taxi back to a different bus station and catch the 12:30 p.m. Mariano bus. He's the driver of the other local bus, a green and white behemoth built no later than 1970. We call the two main local buses by their driver's names, the other being the Lisandro bus. Mariano is very laid back, usually wearing a plaid colored shirt and always willing to help anyone carry their goods – including chickens – on or off the bus. We usually arrive back home at about 1:45 p.m., eat a quick lunch and at 2 p.m. we start our Spanish class with *Professora* Rosibel, normally finishing around 4:30 or 5 p.m. Spanish is coming along *poco a poco* (little by little) – although it feels like vocabulary and grammar have only signed up for short-term rental space in our heads, often vacating the premises as soon as class is over.

The best part of learning comes in those moments of asking for directions, or just sitting in our neighbor Adilsa's front yard and talking about the weather, politics or how good the local *nacatamales* taste (basically the national dish of Nicaragua, delicious corn-tamales filled with shredded pork and vegetables). Inevitably during these conversations, a slice of local life enters in. It's in these moments that we feel somehow more local, more Nicaraguan, like the time thirteen yellow downy ducklings marched confidently by during one deep discussion,

When you live in another country, don't yet speak the language and have new experiences literally every moment, life can be both challenging and really interesting. Once, as we were walking to the bus, our neighbor proudly presented us with two armadillos he had bought at the local market; we didn't even know they had armadillos in Nicaragua! Another time, we went family 'machete' shopping as Olle had been fixated on getting his own knife ever since he saw Don Leonel use a giant one to craft a piece of wood into a handle for our garden hoe. We are working to live as Nicaraguans do, to accept life as it unfolds, regardless of the circumstances in front of us.

Miriam frequently teaches a Pilates-Yoga class to three or four local women after we run in the peanut fields. We sweep off our patio, lay down towels, and soon one can hear grunts and lots of Spanish words describing movement and body parts; *espalda, tocar los pies, estirar las piernas.* Miriam, like the rest of us still lacking in much more than basic Spanish, is using Pilates as a language to connect with others.

Most of our dinners are beans and rice, together with carrots, onions, tomatoes, peppers and garlic. Harlan and Olle are already getting sick of the cuisine, but that's what's for dinner so they just have to get their big boy pants on and eat! Actually, the challenge with anything related to food is the ants. They are so prolific that if you drop one bean, one corner of a cracker, or forgot to sweep up a dead cricket in the corner of a room, they will form a line many yards long and proceed to march to the food until it is all gone. If you leave something really sweet like a jar of honey not closed or hermetically sealed in a Ziploc, those little buggers will find it!

If they don't, either a chicken or one of the many local dogs will. The dogs are not the least worried about breaking into your kitchen even after you've wildly waved a broom and snarled viciously back at them.

Chapter 4:
Grave Digging, Rain Sweeping and Iguana Soup

Early October

There are many different places and spaces that are conducive to writing. Perhaps none more than under a thatch-roof patio, an ever so slight breeze visible in the nearby eucalyptus trees, gnats whispering in your ears and chickens pecking at your toes and coffee!

Garbage day in Nicaragua is more of a mindset than a weekly pick-up. In a small village like El Tololar, there are no sanitation services, so you dig a hole in your backyard. We are now on our third hole, and learning the nuances of waste management. Hole #1 lasted one week (not deep enough). Hole #2 lasted two and one-half weeks (deeper and wider, but not sufficient to handle the amount of garbage created by an American family unaccustomed to living as earth-friendly as locals). Then we dug our third hole: Bingo! It was about the length of a grave – 4 feet deep and 3½ feet wide. Things we learned?

1. After you dump your garbage, throw a little dirt over it to keep the chickens but more importantly the dogs from getting in and spreading garbage all around.

2. Wear closed-toed shoes when digging. This prevents ant bites, which you are guaranteed to get wearing flip flops or bare feet.

3. In addition to a shovel, bring a local tool called a *cova* with you. A *cova* has a long metal handle with a sharp, curved blade at the end. It is perfect (and really essential) for cutting through roots and breaking up hard, volcanic soil.

4. You can burn your garbage. Not the best for the environment maybe, but in a place with no services, you have to make choices. Burning garbage creates more space and keeps pests at bay, and allows more time before you need to dig your next hole.

Schooling for the boys has recently shifted out of necessity. For the first two and a half weeks, we tried to use an excellent online school option called TECCA. One of Cully's good friends was the vice-principal and the curriculum fulfilled the Massachusetts education requirements we had to hit if the boys were going to continue in their same grades when we returned. We loved TECCA, but chose it on the pretense that we would actually have an Internet connection at our house. Alas, a home connection had proved impossible, unless we wished to shell out some $300 a month and construct our own tower to facilitate the connection. And even then we aren't guaranteed it will work. So we are going with the next best thing, or perhaps an even better thing; *Professora* Miriam teaching in our very own two-room schoolhouse. The first couple weeks of teaching went satisfactorily for both Miriam and the boys. Despite never having taught core curriculum subjects in the past, Miriam has proven to be a formidable Science, Language Arts, French, and Social Studies guru.

But educating and learning is a trial for everyone. When we noticed Olle having trouble paying attention because of a case of excessive rocking (we had purchased four rocking chairs when we arrived but had no other places to sit), our friend Beto helped us procure some desks from the local school to quell the shaking. Somehow, in between breaks for swatting wasps and bugs, dodging the smell of chemicals being sprayed on the nearby corn field, sweeping the ever present dust from the rooms, and riding out earthquakes, school and learning are continuing. Education just gets more interesting when sizeable earthquakes hit during Language Arts class on successive weeks, as they did recently.

One recent Sunday we rented a large pick-up truck, loaded up 18 people (15 in the back) and drove more than an hour to a beautiful, mostly secluded, aquamarine, volcanic crater lake. The trip there involved lots of bobbing and weaving for those standing in the bed as we collectively dodged overhanging trees. We made an unexpected detour when one of our participants deemed it of the utmost urgency to find *nacatamales. Nacatamales* are generally eaten on the weekends and the best ones are never served in restaurants but made in small, local kitchens across the country. Alas, after our truck had circumnavigated the town several times and asked at least five villagers where we could find the tasty treats, we were out of luck. Fifteen minutes later we were walking down a steep hill, getting eaten by mosquitoes and wondering if they carried zika or dengue, finally arriving at the picture-perfect lake, crowned by a beautiful deep-green forest with now dormant volcanoes looming overhead. We jumped right in and spent a delicious three hours swimming, eating, and just being together with our family and Nicaraguan friends.

When our Spanish class ends, we normally look for a bit of an escape. Sometimes we all go running in the peanut field together. Other times Harlan plays baseball with his new friends and Olle uses his awesome sense of humor to entertain two 4-year-olds who live nearby. One sunny day, Harlan decided to go running alone. He returned breathing heavily with fantastic stories of monsters chasing him through the field. Apparently near the final turn of the peanut field, he had been accosted by a group of dogs – there are a lot of dogs here. Most of the time they mostly leave you alone and are only interested in scavenging for food, but not always. Harlan made it back safely, a little bit spooked and with only a scratch or two, managing to get back home thanks to his lightning-fast speed. Our new rule is that we never run alone.

Last week was a tough one for Harlan. After a couple weeks of on and off stomach problems, we decided he needed to be seen by someone. Our neighbors were all so willing and ready to help with anything, and before we knew it Cully, Harlan and Beto were riding a motorcycle on curvy dirt roads, dodging chickens and cows on the way to see the doctor. The bumpy ride did not help with Harlan's nausea, but we made it into León without any mishaps.

Getting seen turned out to be a remarkably smooth process. The doctor ushered us into his small office. He asked a few questions in Spanish (Harlan answered in Spanish; way to go dude!), checked his neck, throat and stomach, and quickly prescribed three different medicines. Almost magically, we were able to obtain the pills at the pharmacy, conveniently situated next door, a small window connecting the doctor to the pharmacist. Fifteen bucks later (this included the doctor visit, the medicine, and two orange Gatorades) we were out the door. A few days later, Harlan was fully recovered, at least from that particular bout.

One morning, we woke up at 4:30 a.m. and started loading yucca onto a tractor trailer. It is now the yucca planting season, and we had a chance to participate in the whole process, which goes something like this. First, you take a bunch of yucca branches from the previous year's harvest. With your machete, you cut the long pieces into small chunks, about 4-6 inches each. Each small piece must have at least one shoot (sapling) that will grow into a new yucca plant. You load the small pieces into burlap sacks, and then pile them onto a trailer (most people don't have their own tractors so you need to rent one; it seems that John Deere and Belarusian-made tractors are the most popular). You drive the tractor and trailer to the planting field about 3 km away. En route, you stop at Nestor's grandmother's house to get a plow, and with six or seven people you load the weighty contraption on the trailer.

Once at the field, you unload the yucca and the plow, detach the trailer, and hook the plow to the tractor. Then you load yucca seedlings into blue bins that you tie to the top. The plow (with 3 separate blades) is driven through the field and two guys sit on top of the bins, throwing yucca into the freshly plowed lines. Other people walk behind the tractor, pressing the yucca into the soil with one foot while spreading and pressing down the dirt with the other. Locals (like Aquiles, Carlos, and Franklin) mostly do this barefoot, but due to biting ants (again, they are everywhere) and small, really sharp thorns, shoes are highly recommended.

It was amazing to be a part of the process of how a typical rural family in Nicaragua lives and makes a living. First of all, life is not easy. Average annual income is about $1,200. There is no wiggle room for extras, such as date nights out or weekend trips to the lake. But, people are hyper- efficient with their resources. Miriam was helping our friend Adilsa paint her house one weekend. They finished one room and had a bit of white paint left. Adilsa found a small bit of leftover red paint from a previous job. They mixed the two with extra water and came up with a gorgeous salmon color and enough to paint a solid two-thirds of the bathroom.

For us, rain can be kind of a nuisance, especially when it comes down torrentially. Several times we have found ourselves playing the 'sweeping' game, taking turns with the broom, headlights affixed, and pushing water away from the rooms into the field. During a heavy storm the broom technique barely keeps up with the rain. When it's windy, rain pushes through the windows and into the rooms. This water is hard to sweep as there is a divider between the room and the patio, and you just have to pray the wind stops. For the people in El Tololar, rain is everything. They get plenty of sun but in the rainy season – May through October – they really need a lot of precipitation. Climate change has been shifting weather patterns and even though September and October seemed very wet, in reality they are way behind on their totals for the season. On days the sky is blue, we hope and pray that the storm clouds, visible on the distant horizon, will rise and pour again.

The pillars that hold up the palm roof of our patio are homes to lots of creatures. One day, we noticed termites had started eating into the beams, joining the wasps that were chewing a few weeks earlier. We asked our friend Wilmar what we should do. He said his house has thousands of termites but that there is no possibility of structural damage. What a relief!

Our kitten 'Dulce, or Sweetie', is great at climbing the same wooden columns. But she isn't so good at getting down. In the absence of an unexpected and major demolition success by the termites, we will continue to need to help scaredy-cat down.

When you are learning another language but don't yet know a lot, signs can be particularly confusing. One day we saw a sign advertising, "*zapatos* (shoes), *ortopedia* (shoe inserts) and *tacos*." Upon further review t*acos* are the name for the heel of a shoe, but when seen during a lunchtime walk the sign can be a bit confusing. The same goes for the word *verdugo*. It was written on a sign at what looked like a shopping mall, super market-type place. A quick consult of the dictionary showed *verdugo* to have several meanings, including executioner, hangman, cruel person and tyrant. We haven't found another definition and thus may need to drive by the strip mall for further investigation.

Grass and weeds grow quickly in El Tololar and in just one month our yard has gone from a mostly dirt field used primarily for horse grazing and baseball games to an overgrown plot with corn, nascent vegetable sprouts, garbage holes, and lots of weeds. We don't have a goat or a lawnmower (although we do at times have an adopted large, hairy pink pig) so Miriam and Cully recently borrowed Olle's machete – it's up for debate why we allowed a nine-year-old easy access to a machete in the first place – and spent part of several afternoons 'mowing' the lawn. This was achieved by bending down and whacking the weeds with a sideways motion taught to us by our next-door neighbor Aquiles. We quickly found it is not wise to kneel on the ground while you whack; Cully received no less than thirty ant bites on his left leg during one particularly brisk chopping session.

Don Leonel owns several of the white horses that hang out in the local environs. Recently, Olle got it in his head that he wanted to ride one (or all) of the horses. When he gets something in his mind, watch out! Several follow-up conversations led us to believe that a specific Wednesday afternoon at around 4 p.m. would in fact be the best time to ride. Starting at 2 p.m., Olle began running over to Don Leonel's house every 10 minutes to see if the horses were there. It turns out that several of the horses had decided to 'go rogue' and had last been seen walking and grazing down the road in the company of a larger group. Olle couldn't wait, setting off down the dirt road and coming upon Don Leonel leading the horses back home. The fact that he didn't have a saddle handy didn't faze Olle, who wasted no time mounting a particularly boney horse, grinning ear to ear. He rode the horse (named something like "lightning fast") home, where Miriam also turned out to be a pro, taking a couple expert loops around the yard.

We often walk to our friend Ivania's home to play with her baby rabbits. While there we talk about the possibility of someday eating iguana soup (they had a lot of iguanas in the trees behind their house) and discuss with Ivania and her family about their life. They are a delightful family who like many, live on the edge economically. Every day Ivania wakes up early and makes food (tacos, salad, enchiladas, fresh fruit drinks) that she sells to students at the local secondary school. Normally she takes her wares on a wagon hauled by her almost completely blind horse. However, during one of our chats she told us that her horse had eaten yucca (eating yucca stalks can, it turns out, be very dangerous for some horses) and quite suddenly died. This was actually a huge blow to her family, as transportation to the school is vital to their livelihood. She began borrowing or "renting" a horse but there is an additional cost to this that is difficult for a family to bear. But somehow she grins and bears it and perseveres, because she must.

Chapter 5:

The Corn King, Chili Adventures, A Doctor is Born

Mid/Late October

Carlos knows his corn – like, really knows it. Our neighbor Carlos and his wife Miriam live kitty-corner across from us – our houses separated by a field of weeds, two barbed-wire fence crossings, one pig, two chicken coops, and a latrine. As far as we know, our home will go to Carlos and Miriam when we leave, as it sits on their property. When we arrived, one-inch high corn seedlings were barely visible in the field that surrounds our house. Six weeks later, the corn stands six feet high and takes up an area of about forty by twenty yards, situated stage-right as you look out from our thatched-roof patio.

It is a pretty small cornfield by local standards, but provides enough corn for Carlos and Miriam to feed their animals for a part of the year, and make local corn tortillas and other maize-based culinary delights. Miriam works as a teacher at the local secondary school, a 25-minute walk from our house by the local road, a 20-minute walk by shortcut through the volcano-framed peanut field, or a 10-minute bus ride – depending on how much it rained the night before. Teachers (like everyone who lives in the village and not unlike teachers in the US) are paid a paltry amount when compared to the incredibly important role they play in cultivating the lives of children. Miriam is the family's principle breadwinner, and Carlos tends the garden during the growing season and finds odd jobs (often hired for his expert machete skills to clear land).

They live on the edge and like most people, don't have extras for any entertainment or additional education or job-training opportunities. Miriam has three children from a previous marriage – three beautiful daughters aged ten, twelve, and thirteen – and if she ever has any spare funds, it goes directly to those girls. Family is all important in Nicaragua. But the dynamics can be very different than the United States. For example, Miriam is fifteen years older than Carlos. In Nicaragua, it is very common, in fact, for older women to have a much younger partner; it is usually the women who hold the full-time job. When we recently divulged that we had been married for 13 years, most people were floored.

But damn, Carlos knows his corn. One day, he asked to borrow some of the chemical we had recently purchased to murder (that's a bit harsh: exterminate) the biting ants that are ever-present in the volcanic soil that surrounds our house. Apparently said chemical also works on worms (and wasps, spiders, various beetles) that can lay eggs in and eat the corn. Carlos probably has about 1,000 stalks of corn. We said he could borrow as much chemical as he wanted, but he said he only needed it for one stalk. We walked over with him and sure enough, down in between the leaves of one stalk were tens of tiny worm eggs. He sprayed the chemical and handed back the bottle. Only one stalk had eggs (out of 1,000 plus), he knew it, and that was all he required.

Our house is situated on Miriam Rivas's property and the larger area includes houses for much of the patriarch's, Don

Leonel's, family. There are seven houses on the larger property, and an amazing array of fruit trees, especially at Don Leonel's. He has a huge grapefruit tree you can climb and "shake" fruit from whenever you have a craving. He also has at least two types of *guayaba* tree (one with a fruit most comparable in size to an apple but much tarter, the other with small, greenish-yellow skin and a pink, seedy, inside). We haven't yet taken a real liking to either. There are many other trees in his yard, including a *nancita* tree (with really small, tart yellow fruit that all came down at the same time a week ago), a coconut tree, and at least ten papaya trees. Don Leonel said the papayas will be ready at the end of November and December. Some of the green fruit are huge and for our taste buds, December can't come soon enough to try them.

Using the bathroom(s) near our house is always an experience. We generally have three choices:

1. The actual bathroom at our neighbor Adilsa's house: Replete with lighting, a sit-down toilet, a sink, and soap. Adilsa said we could use her bathroom anytime, but she often has a lot of people staying there and at times it seems like an imposition, plus the water doesn't always run.

2. The latrine at Miriam and Carlos's house: Of the two latrines it is the closest to our house and generally the cleanest. But, it sits in the open without any bushes or trees for privacy. At night it is ok if you have a headlamp, don't mind walking near the pig and make sure to not look down the hole, but during the day the door opens in full view of a hammock that Miriam and Carlos often frequent in the afternoons. Especially when they have visitors, it takes a lot of courage to walk over, say "Hola,"

enter the latrine and then exit soon thereafter to a group of smiling faces.

3. The latrine at Wilmar's: From the outside it looks just like Miriam's and has the advantage of being semi-secluded by small trees. It seemed like the best option when we arrived and even had a broom to sweep the floor when needed. However, during one sweeping session we found that the handle was infested with termites, making the Miriam-Carlos latrine the clear front-runner, at least for now.

The bus stop near our house can be pretty muddy, especially during or right after a rainstorm. That wouldn't be so bad but the mud is usually mixed with loads of cow poop, and squishy mangoes from the trees overhead. This makes the intersection a haunt of various pigs (big and small), most of whom have two-pieces of wood forming an X around their neck as a way to keep them from breaking through a neighbor's fence and eating their corn. Sometimes, after a really heavy downpour, the pigs like to wallow in the muddy, poopy bus tracks that form in the center of the road. Getting to the bus stop involves taking a shortcut through the fence at the corner of Carlos's corn, then walking down a dirt-road with knee-high weeds, a fair bit of horse chips, the occasional iguana or small gecko, ants (always) and depending on the day, either one or two of Don Leonel's emaciated white horses. There is another barbed-wire fence at the end of the short cut that is pretty low but can be a challenge to get over without ripping your grocery bags when returning by bus from a León shopping trip.

One weekend we came home from a walk. Olle needed to use the bathroom, and Cully needed to go buy eggs at the *venta.* As we came to the bus stop intersection, about fifty cows were walking past, heading to a nearby field to graze. We were definitely at a crossroads, as we needed eggs (one direction) but Olle really had to use the facilities (a different route). Our compromise was that Cully would get eggs, and Olle would wait till the last cow passed (a calf), and then follow behind him until he came to the bathroom trail. Somewhere we have a great photo of a nine-year-old following the herd.

Sometimes, no matter what your life is like, you need distractions. We brought the game 'UNO' with us from the States and it was unknown in Nicaragua. Maybe someday 'ONE' will catch on back home. *Bananagrams* (the Spanish-version) was also new to our neighbors and we have played several games, losing quite badly as expected but at times managing to write words like *taco* and *bueno.*

Fruit, like a lot of things on the property, is sort of communal. You can pick a *guayaba* whenever you want from anyone's trees and they are more than happy to share. If you get a craving for a specific flavor, it seems that there is always a bush or tree to match; take spiciness. One Sunday, Adilsa showed us a small bush not far from Wilmar's latrine with tiny green, orange and red chilies. The red ones were ripe, and as Harlan found out the hard way, despite their size they should not be chewed and swallowed directly unless you are looking for stomach pains for multiple hours afterward. Picking the chilies also requires care, and on several occasions while picking we have found ourselves standing in the middle of a long, line of biting ants.

We met a woman named Maria just before church a few weeks after we arrived (during a memorial service for a woman who had died seven months prior). She was incredibly sweet and said that after the service we had to stop by her house and try *repochetas*. At the time we didn't know what a *repocheta* was but were eager to try a new local culinary delight. We were a bit tired and had been prepared to go home directly after the service for several reasons. First, Miriam and Olle had been eaten by mosquitoes while Adilsa introduced us to one of several local types of pear trees prior to the start of the service. Second, we had just sat through a long, very hot, two hour service in Spanish that included multiple flybys by bats at the front of the sanctuary, no breeze whatsoever under the tin-roof building, and thirty-plus sessions of rising and sitting, rising and sitting with the rest of the congregation. Lastly, the chili pepper Harlan had decided to eat on our way to church had begun to take its effect and the regularity of the noises coming from his stomach was accelerating.

We arrived at Maria's house and instantly recognized it as the place the Lisandro bus often stops to allow the *cobrador* (the guy who collects money on the bus) to get off and order tortillas with *cuajada. Cuajada* is a local, homemade salty cheese that can be bought from a family on motorcycle who comes near our house weekly, or from one of the many small markets or *ventas* that many people set up in their house as a way to make a little extra money. *Cuajada* is a bit of an acquired taste, but doesn't need to be instantly refrigerated and we have found it to be a delicious accompaniment and much-appreciated addition to the daily meals of rice and beans.

Maria and her daughter sat and talked with us (they were absolutely smitten with Harlan and Olle) while the daughter's husband Carlos made us *repochetas*, deep fried tortillas filled with creamy and crispy *cuajada* and topped with more, locally made white cream sauce. They brought out cups of soda (Harlan had taken a liking to a local, bright red soda called Rojita, generally considered by the rest of the family to be the worst soda ever made) and plates of piping hot *repochetas*, Harlan's stomach improved markedly after the meal, likely no thanks to the *Rojita*. Our family decided then and there that our new favorite food are *repochetas*. We looked forward to purchasing the ingredients from Maria in the hopes that we could recreate Carlos's delicious, cheesy treat. We tried and unfortunately, our version doesn't even come close

Food in Nicaragua can be a love-hate kind of thing. It is easy to love rice and beans, and it is equally easy to be a bit sick of them after five straight meals. *Nacatamales* are different and a less-frequent treat (at least for Miriam and Cully -Harlan and Olle have not warmed up to them). One Saturday, the *nacatamale* guy sold his food off the back of a truck with a loudspeaker. Another time, his truck must have been in the shop. But that didn't stop him. At 5:45 a.m. he showed up on the edge of our yard, without a speaker but with a voice loud enough to know what he was selling. That time he was on horseback and wearing a red and white apron, the *nacatamales* wrapped in banana leaves strapped to the side. Miriam and Cully were already up with the chickens doing exercises and it didn't take much prodding to find 60 *cordobas* (about 2 dollars) to order two giant *nacatamales* to be put aside for dinner.

Living in Nicaragua, you really came to like, or dislike, lizards. There are green and black iguanas that hang out in the trees and wood piles of some of our neighbors, and then the hundreds of smaller, gecko-type lizards. They generally spend most of their time in the rafters and mind their own business, eating a steady diet of spiders, gnats, moths, flies, and other insects that would otherwise have had the run of the house. They don't usually come down to the floor level, thanks in large part to our adopted cat, *Dulce,* who supplements her morning cat food with crickets at night and lizards during the day. Normally you know when a lizard is above you in two ways. First, they make a pretty loud but soothing clicking noise. Second, they defecate with great regularity and it isn't uncommon for *Familia Lundgren* to be targeted by a 'gecko-bomb.'

The water-flow challenges at our house have begun increasing, in line with the arrival of October, the wettest of the rainy months. In general, the small rain and thunderstorms that pop up most afternoons are not a problem if the rain comes down slowly; October brought more deluges though. The rain-sweeping we do as a team helps, but generally fails to keep the water from entering our bedroom. If the rain is really heavy, there is a spot in the ceiling in each of the bedrooms that leaks onto the beds. To address the leaks, one day Aquiles, Wilmar, and Beto came over to help install a gutter system on the edge of the roof. After several attempts at shifting the angle of the gutter (basically a piece of sheet metal bent to the correct shape), a nasty looking lightning storm appeared on the horizon and dropped all we needed and more to test the new system. So far their adjustment has been a success, at least until the December windy season arrives and turns the gutters into flying projectiles.

We have great friends and during our year in Nicaragua they have been helpful in so many ways. During our first six weeks, we did dishes outside, in the same sink we used to wash our clothes. That is not normal, but it just took a while to get a kitchen sink up and running (because you didn't buy but rather build your sink). For two days, our friend and neighbor Aquiles worked tirelessly to build us an actual sink inside our kitchen.

Sinks stations are made from scratch and except for the aluminum sink itself, Aquiles built the whole foundation. He built two brick walls on either side of the faucet, then put a layer of cement over those. For the top, he used pieces of rebar and a wood frame to build the space where the sink would sit. He used a cool local tool called a *caliche* to pour cement in hard to reach areas and then dug a hole in the brick wall for the water from the pipe to flow outside. Wala! We finally had a sink; no more late-night dishwashing sessions in the great outdoors.

Miriam has intermittently played all sorts of roles during our stay: cook, clothes launderer, Pilates/Yoga instructor, gardener, soccer and baseball player, etc. In another life she also could have easily been a doctor or a nurse, as she proved one Saturday afternoon. A soccer game had just started at Don Leonel's. Not five minutes in, Miriam came walking down the path with her hand on Leo's head. Leo, one of Harlan and Olle's best friends, had run into the low roof that juts out from the corner of Don Leonel's house. He had a small but rather deep gash on the top of his head, and it was pretty bloody. Miriam took charge, ordered people to run and get hydrogen peroxide, gauze pads, Band-Aids, and antibiotic ointment. She was cool as a cucumber, keeping both Leo and his Mom calm. In the end it was agreed that stitches were not necessary and that liquid Band-Aid and a slight shave of the head would work the best. Leo didn't participate in the rest of the soccer match – which turned out to be a marathon, two-hour affair – but he was ready to go the next day thanks to Miriam.

On weekend mornings, most of our neighbors take it a bit slower than usual, perhaps even sleeping in till 6 a.m. We often mimic that pace of life, and one recent lazy Saturday we rolled out of bed late, just before six. We were hoping to have neighbors over to watch a movie on our patio, and Miriam began making six batches of popcorn for the twilight showing. Two of the popcorn bags were subsequently eaten by one of the many, oft annoying, dogs that frequent the area (and our kitchen if we don't lock it).

Carlos came over early to start 'machete-ing' the lawn, the best way to keep your grass short in lieu of mowers or a ready supply of goats. Every bit of work is helpful to he and Miriam, and we make it a habit to pay him for the six hours of work it takes to chop our grass. Harlan and Olle spent much of the day playing next-door with Leo. We did laundry, chatted, and got ready for soccer. The rain came down in force later in the day, which made all the farmers happy, but resulted in the cancellation of movie night. Carlos walked over again in the afternoon, checking his corn for worms, diligent as ever. What a wondrously ordinary day it was.

CORN UPDATE: We had a very rapid but strong thunderstorm come through at about 5 p.m. a few nights back. The entire storm only lasted 20 minutes or so but for a hairy five minutes the wind was intense, our two hammocks swinging around and around like pinwheels. Miriam spent the storm next door at Adilsa's as she got caught there while helping Adilsa bring her clothes in from the line. The tall corn near our house suffered the most, a large swath of it bending steeply towards our house. Carlos was out checking it even before the storm ended.

The initial diagnosis was not good, and there were fears that a fair bit of the crop may have been lost. But the next day, there was Carlos, tenderly attending to each stalk. He took a shovel, pulled up nearby dirt, patted it around the base of each stalk, and pressed it down with his feet. That, plus a bright sun, helped most of his corn to rise again. In fact, that one storm knocked corn over all across the region. During the following days, our family had the chance to participate in helping to give new life to corn, one stalk at a time. We helped in Don Leonel's field, wearing long sleeves to avoid being cut by the sharp corn leaves. It felt good to help, and it was a powerful education for all of us, to understand viscerally how close our Nicaraguan family lives to nature, and to the edge of having and wanting.

Chapter 6:

The Purpose, Chicken Soup, Snake Charming

Late October

A Poem by Cully

Through the shattered glass of grass and
weed, visions emerge

Souls are animated, the heights call to all,
bending their ear for the morning dirge

We sway in the wind, rain, sun and we rise

Again, riding the unexpected, all is ethereal

Weeks tick-tock, searching for the nearest
purpose, the moments reveal

Why are we here? What is our purpose? These are existential questions that we often ask ourselves, no matter where we live. In Nicaragua, this topic certainly comes up for us quite a lot. It is hard at times to hold in tension the fact that we want to learn so much and yet have been there less than two months. Our Spanish is improving but still has a long way to go, and it has taken a while to settle in to the rhythm of our daily life. We tell ourselves we need to have grace for each other and some more time to get acclimated, but still, this whole purpose thing keeps tugging at us.

But purpose often clarifies itself over time and space, and both are coming into better view, thanks to a bit of faith, and the vision of our Nicaraguan friends for a better life and more opportunities for the community of El Tololar. One recent Friday we held a skype call with Tyler St. Claire, the Executive Director of Tololamos. The next day, we had a great meeting with Adilsa, Beto and Wilmar, the three main on-the-ground staff of Tololamos. Sometimes meetings, like great ideas, can't happen until the time is right for a variety of reasons. That Saturday's meeting would have been tough to hold much sooner for one key reason; Beto, Wilmar and Adilsa don't speak English. Holding it on the first month would have been fruitless. Even after two months, it was a challenge. But on October 22nd, 2016 for one hour, we held a meeting in Spanish; the awesome thing is that we understood the meeting's content – at least we think we did.

The meeting's participants included Miriam, Cully, Beto, Adilsa and Wilmar and centered on three areas of greatest need on which Tololamos wants to focus in the upcoming months – health, education, and agriculture. Within these three sectors, they outlined several specific projects they want to implement. They are modest projects that look to address real, immediate needs. And the great thing is, for a small investment, lives can be changed. For example, the local health clinic does an amazing job trying to address the needs of the entire community. They do their best with what they have, and would benefit greatly from larger investments. These include an ambulance to bring patients to the hospitals in León, a qualified pediatrician to address the health needs of hundreds and hundreds of children, and access to medical supplies and better medical equipment. But to start, their needs are more basic. They need chairs for waiting patients and mothers with babies to sit on, new lights to replace old ones, tools and a few parts to fix broken sinks, and a couple of fans to help sick people feel a little cooler during the hot, dusty, summer months. All these little interventions can make a big difference, and for only about 300 dollars.

In our meeting we talked more about providing scholarships for students, fixing water systems, and building fences to keep chickens, cows and horses from eating valuable crops. We also talked about the ways we might be able to help the community unite around some of these issues, because purpose is only possible with people.

We run in the beautiful peanut fields many evenings, bouncing through verdant green leaves, the plants accentuated by tiny yellow flowers. Huge volcanoes shrouded by smoke rise above us. We run by horses nibbling at the edges of the field, their heads stretched through the barbed-wire, trying to reach the most delicious leaves. It is beautiful, and for a moment when we run, we forget the challenges of ant bites, days without running water, nighttime latrine runs, gnats in most orifices, cow-pooped stained roads, and so much humidity that it takes only hours for mold to grow on the inside of our bedroom doors. When we run, we are transported to another place and it helps remind us of the beauty of Nicaragua and its people.

But the peanuts are, ala Charles Dickens, a tale of two plants. One is our perception of the nut when we run, the other is how it directly impacts people's lives.

In a nutshell, large peanut agribusinesses, whose product is usually destined for export, come to villages like Tololar to look for farmers who will rent them their land. Many Nicaraguan farmers are having more and more difficulty making ends meet by planting traditional crops such as yucca, potatoes, and peppers, a result of both changing rain patterns and a national economy that remains the second poorest in the Western Hemisphere. Hence renting land out provides farmers with at least a modicum of income, though they receive a paltry sum even by local standards. What's worse is what the businesses do once they have access to the land. In short, they spray a ton of chemicals (always at night – it took us a while to figure out what that sweet, acidic smell is that wafts across our patio from time to time). The chemicals keep the fields free of weeds and looking gorgeous for our evening runs. They also destroy the soil and are suspected to be the cause of an increase in kidney issues among children and others in the community. And even if a farmer decides to stop renting his land for peanuts, it takes up to two years for the soil to regenerate to a place where other crops can be grown again.

Today it is peanuts. Twenty years ago it was cotton, which according to stories we have been told was much worse. At that time, the same general system was in place; large agribusinesses, small-holder farmers, economic needs at the local level vs. a search for the largest profits and the lowest costs. The difference in the 80s and 90s was that growing cotton produced different detrimental health and environmental impacts. Back then, they didn't just use a tractor and a machine to spray chemicals. They used airplanes. The planes were very efficient in several ways. They helped create bumper, weed-free crops of cotton. They were also effective in a collateral way. People got really sick; birds, cows and horses fell over, dead. Animals are like a walking bank-account for rural Nicaraguans and when they die, you can't make a withdrawal. It was a huge problem that brought the community together. The cotton businesses left, the planes stopped making fly-bys. For a time, things were back to normal. For a time…

Previously we told the story of Ivania and her blind horse that had died from eating yucca. Death by yucca is a relatively rare occurrence, but a misfortune that resulted in a serious economic hit to the family. The horse had been responsible for pulling a load of food and drinks, prepared every morning, to be sold at the local secondary school. Good news: thanks to the support of our family and friends, Ivania and her husband Denis now have a new horse named Roseo. Roseo is brown with mottled white marks. He is a bit skittish and it may take a while for him to get comfortable pulling the food cart. He's a horse of a different color, but he's a horse nonetheless and hopefully will be pulling loads of delicious food (food that Harlan and Olle have sampled and love) to the school for many years.

Rainer is white and fluffy. She (we think that is her gender) has gorgeous pink eyes. She will eat anything, but seems to prefer green leaves and chewing the wood that composes the frame of her fenced-in enclosure. She has become fast friends with our kitten Dulce, although for a time Dulce seemed to be hunting her incessantly. Now they just play together on either side of the fence. Rainer was a gift to us from Ivania and Denis and Olle has been pining for a rabbit since he first saw them in their hutches underneath Denis's iguana-laden trees soon after we arrived. Rainer got her name by virtue of her coming to us in the middle of a torrential downpour. She now has an outdoor enclosure, thanks to Wilmar and Carlos's help. For nighttime, we purchased a small *jaula* (hutch) where Rainer sleeps, usually in our kitchen. While purchasing the *jaula*, Cully was given an exclusive, inside tour of the home that stood behind the storefront, where various cages held one fat rabbit, six really aggressive parrots, and two most likely illegal but very cute Capuchin monkeys.

During the same downpour that brought us Rainer, the water brought out other even more exotic animals. We were walking back home with Rainer snuggled under Miriam's raincoat, the dirt road having turned into a small river with various tributaries jutting off toward this or that person's home. Wilmar was walking in the lead on the right side of the road. Suddenly, he jumped to one side, barely dodging a seven-foot boa constrictor slithering through a puddle. Upon closer examination, the boa had been run over near his back end by a vehicle, most likely either the Lisandro bus which had just passed, or possibly one of the ubiquitous motorcycles (generally 125 horsepower) that ply the roads of El Tololar. He (or she) was definitely still alive and energetic enough that we only stopped long enough to take a few photos with zoom on high! According to Wilmar, boa sightings are rare and he hadn't seen one in years. This is partially because when people encounter a boa, they usually eat it. He also said that since the boa only got run over near the tail, there is a good chance that he will go on to slither another day.

Weekends are a great break from school for both Miriam and the boys. It may be hard to imagine, but holding school five days a week in the two rooms of our small house plus our patio is really tough. It is hard to focus with the bugs and the heat, and interaction with fellow students is a sorely missed part of the day. But there are elements of the boys' education that they would never get at home, like when Miriam was teaching Olle social studies last week and was able to expertly weave into his learning the real-life challenges of the peanut business, pesticides, and impacts on the local environment from an economic and social perspective. But the break that weekends provide necessitate that the boys be creative with how they spend their time. Especially during the heat of the day when it is too hot to go outside and most people lay low from 10 a.m. – 3 p.m., it can be a challenge to stay entertained.

Recently, Harlan and Olle, on their own initiative, addressed this issue head-on. Taking a page from the Lemonade-Stand playbook, they made popcorn (*palomita de maiz*) and juice (*fresca*) squeezed from fresh grapefruits, local peaches (*melacotóns*), and lemons (okay, they had some help from Miriam). Their business plan evolved over the course of an hour and they ultimately decided to go door to door rather than expecting their clients to come to them. With a large bowl each of popcorn and fruit juice, they went from house to house (or hammock to hammock) to each of our neighbors, charging one *cordoba* (about 3 cents) for each product, provided that each customer supplied their own cup and plate. Everyone bought some, a few people even buying seconds. The boys learned a lot from their business venture, but more importantly it was a really creative way to connect and enter into conversation with our friends. In many ways they were helping to live out our purpose here, to find deeper meaning in relationships with others.

The morning cacophony of crickets chirping in our rooms, Dulce meowing outside our door, roosters crowing in the surrounding yards and the distant honking of buses and trucks usually begins around 3:30 a.m., although some roosters seem to go all night and the cricket decibel level ramps up as dawn approaches. The only element of this noise we have control over is Dulce, and we switched to feeding her at night in the hopes that her stomach would stop telling her to meow quite so early. The results of the experiment are still pending, and we are definitely in the market for a good vendor selling cricket muzzles. But the noises are a part of life, even the trucks, and we are growing accustomed to listening and learning from them. But why they need to honk at 4:00 a.m., when there are no other cars on the road and the cows and chickens haven't yet started using them for the day as thoroughfares, is a mystery to us.

Showers are a necessity when you live in the village and we are told that once the dry season really kicks in during March and April, multiple showers a day will be a requirement because of the extreme amount of dust that gets kicked up with every step one takes. Our outdoor shower is pretty basic even by local standards. It's connected to our kitchen and made from brick and mortar with walls about six feet plus high and a concrete floor. Some grass grows inside, and at nighttime you really need two headlamps, placed on either side of the wall, to provide adequate lighting. The only problem with the lights is that they attract all sorts of weird flying things. Day showers can be nice and more comfortable than night showers in the rain, as long as you can dodge the wasps that fly in and out of the water streams.

For three full days last week, we had no water. But Adilsa our neighbor has a shower that sources its water from a well, not the municipal water source, so she usually has water for showers when we don't. One day Olle took the first shower at Adilsa's, and had a solid stream. Harlan and Cully were next and managed to have enough flow to rinse off the soap, barely, although it seemed like the decline in pressure was a fluke as that had never happened before.

Miriam's shower started great, but quickly turned into a drip, drip, and then nothing. She was left in a predicament; stand there and wait, or put clean clothes over soapy skin and return to our house in the hopes that we had enough water in our 5-gallon bucket to complete the process. She wisely took option b, and thankfully was able to finish the job in our shower. To make the process more efficient, she used our purple bowl to rinse, a container that only an hour earlier had contained the delicious chicken soup she had made for our neighbor Miriam. Miriam had just returned home from a successful gallbladder surgery that found 21 stones, which we all had the privilege to see one evening, all wrapped neatly in a plastic bag.

Ventas are basically rooms in people's houses out of which they sell stuff to make a little extra money. Each *venta* is a little different but most offer basic staples (rice, beans, eggs, a few fruits and vegetables) as well as various other items someone might need in a pinch (coke, beer, hammocks, mouse traps and peanuts). Not everyone has a *venta*, but a lot of people do. We wish they had such stores back home. They are a great way to see someone else's life, to shop and chat, to build relationships and purchase goods at the same time. In this way, the transaction become not only about money, but learning something new about another person each time you make an early morning tortilla run, or just needed *frijoles* because honestly, who can live without *frijoles*?

Our tank of propane for our three-burner stove that worked overtime cooking rice and beans ran out of gas suddenly last week. At first we thought we were in a bit of a pickle, as raw beans and rice just don't cut it and our burners do all our cooking. We had been told that the only place to refill was in León, a 45-minute bus-ride away. It is a reasonable hassle to carry a large tank on the bus, through the crowded city streets and to a gas-refiller guy, and back. But after a conversation with the experts (Carlos, Nelson, Aquiles, and

Wilmar) who were hanging out in our yard at the beginning of Spanish class, we found that in fact there was a propane *hombre* much closer. Carlos offered to borrow Adilsa's motorcycle and take Cully on the back. In addition to being a corn aficionado, Carlos is an expert biker, maneuvering adeptly through the slippery, volcanic soil better than just about anybody. We were at the tail end of another afternoon rain storm but that didn't deter Carlos. With the tank behind him and Cully behind the tank, they made the round-trip journey post-haste. There were only one or two instances of potential danger when Cully's feet flew off the foot pegs while trying to balance his butt on the end of the seat while holding the tank in place.

Chapter 7:
Local Ingenuity, Vampire Bats, and Patience

Early November

It is amazing what can be accomplished with one tool, like a machete, for instance. Since we've been in Nicaragua, we have seen a machete being used alternately as a lawn mower, bottle opener, screwdriver, brick slicer, yucca cutter, coconut chopper, extension cord fixer (not recommended), trailblazer, mango peeler, and many more. Necessity is the mother of invention and indeed we have never come across people who are more resourceful and creative than Nicaraguans. You use what you have and if something breaks, you don't just buy a new one, you fix it.

Aquile's TV went on the fritz last week and on a walk to Don Leonel's house, Cully came across Nestor, Wilmar and Chepe opening up the TV to fix a broken part (with both a screwdriver AND a machete). They were successful in fixing the TV and a little while later, Carlos's mini-speaker system, which was playing a heavily garbled rendition of *La Cucaracha.* We are also amazed by the adaptability of people here. One minute they are in the field planting yucca or plowing a field in the traditional way, with a wooden plow behind two giant bulls. The next they are fixing TVs, computers and cell phones under a giant grapefruit tree.

This local ingenuity plays itself out day after day in many ways. Last week Harlan, Olle and Cully jumped on Nestor's rented tractor with Nestor, Aquiles, Jose and Franklin.

Franklin lives sort of across the street from us. He's exceedingly nice but owns like ten dogs, several of whom seem to accost us every time we do our peanut runs. We fit seven of us on the tractor, Harlan and Olle sitting on top of six or seven sharp machetes that had been brought to cut yucca for planting the next day. Both their butts arrived without so much as a slice, and upon arrival we were treated to a Gilligan's Island-style three-hour tour of Raul's (Nestor's Dad) vast property, peppered with more fruit trees than we'd ever seen, including exotic fruits like the *guanabana*. The tour ended and we parted ways with Raul, who had a potential buyer for his bull arrive near his paddock just as we were getting ready to leave. We were prepared to hop on the tractor for the return trip, but were informed the old John Deere (like, really old) required a jump start. With six of us at the rear and Nestor at the helm, on the count of three we pushed the giant tires forward down the slight incline, Harlan and Olle's muscles bulging just as Nestor popped the clutch and the engine roared to life. That tractor would have been put out to pasture many moons ago in the United States. In Nicaragua, due to a combination of creativity and necessity, it was middle-aged. The seven of us rode home with the smoky sunset bouncing behind us.

It's snowing. The sun is rising and it's already hot at 8:30 a.m. There is a fine, white film on the computer and on the surrounding, rust-colored floor. For a moment, we are transported back to Boston, experiencing our first snowflakes of the year. The sweat beginning to drip down our faces, the butterflies gliding above the corn, and Miriam washing clothes in a tank-top bring us back to reality. The Nicaraguan snowstorm is just the termites at work in the rafters above us.

We came across two really cool creatures this past week. The first was a hummingbird moth, which at first glance is not even distinguishable from its namesake. When resting, it is an enormous moth, about the size of your thumb to index finger when spread apart. It's really beautiful, especially for a moth, mostly a coffee-brown with white stripes accentuated by black lines. When it flies, it instantaneously transforms into a hummingbird, the same size and moving from flower to flower (or chair to chair), dodging and darting in and out. Amazing! The other animal was a small lizard-newt-skink type amphibian with beautiful green and blue accents that none of our neighbors had ever seen before. We only saw it because a woman waiting for a ride from the bus pointed it out of curiosity, and for ten minutes we attempted to snap photos while trying to track her through the roadside weeds.

Miriam finally has her garden. We hope and pray we will see tomatoes, lettuce, peppers, jalapenos, carrots and onions really soon. And if Miriam's dedication is an indication, the crop will be bumper. It took a while to get up and running because we needed to get the chicken-wire for the fence, which required a separate ride on the Mariano bus. We finally procured it and one morning, Carlos and Aquiles helped Cully build a fence for the small *huerta* (garden plot). We wondered where they would get the wood for the fence posts. It turns out you just take a machete to most any tree you can find that has straight limbs, chop it off, de-leaf it and voila, you have your post. We were a bit hesitant to go off hacking into our neighbor's trees but Carlos saw no problem with the idea. He had no problem because in Nicaragua, there is much less a sense of personal ownership, and a more generous understanding that property (including trees) is communal.

In equatorial-type climates, everything grows really fast so we're trusting that other nearby saplings will become trees soon, replacing the trees Carlos chopped. The rest of the garden prep included a lot of hoeing under a hot sun by Miriam and thankfully only three wheelbarrow loads of manure by Harlan and Cully from Esteban's cow paddock. The only problem with using Esteban's poop as fertilizer is that our garden's proximity to our patio may be a cause for the *mosca* (fly) population around our house doubling overnight. We have been deploying new and inventive techniques to deal with the flies, but to no avail.

Our new friend Fernando, who lives down the street, recently introduced us to *jicaro* carvings. *Jicaro* is a fruit that comes in many varieties. One type produces a hard shell that can be hollowed out, dried, and then painted or carved. Fernando showed up at the edge of our yard one rainy-evening with a backpack full of beautiful, *jicaro*-carved bowls, cups, and vases. He had clearly spent time crafting these, and we felt so blessed for his generosity. It was hospitality and friendship in action, and it was a great reminder of how small, intentional actions help bind us all together, no matter where we are. He was hard to convince, but we gave him some money as a thank you. It wasn't a lot, but he had spent many hours carving these beautiful pieces of art (including one shaped and colored like a pumpkin for Halloween) and small investments go a long way to help out people like Fernando.

Mourning doves, early morning hikes and sweet rice pudding have all taken their turn as welcome reminders of home. Miriam and Cully's morning quiet/exercise time on the patio (5:15 – 6:00 a.m. most mornings) is usually set against a backdrop of the sun rising, roosters crowing, gnats waking and mourning doves cooing. Our *jicaro* friend Fernando followed up his first act with another, unannounced drop-by, this time with a delicious, rice pudding (according to some of us) made lovingly by his Mom whom we have yet to meet, with milk, sugar and rice. It was topped with a cinnamon, which at first inhale instantly transported us to the kitchen table at GG's house (Miriam's grandmother) on a crisp fall day, about to dig into a warm slice of apple pie and a scoop of ice cream.

This past weekend, we arose at 4:45 a.m. and walked thirty minutes with Adilsa and Yader to the corner where we caught the Mario bus (not to be confused with the Mariano bus) to the base of Rota, a now extinct volcano mountain with lush fields of corn, red and white beans, coffee and bananas scattered across the mostly flat crater top.

Hiking Rota reminded us of home because we are a hiking family back in Massachusetts. But the experience was unique in several ways. Yader, Fernando's brother and a 19 year-old college student studying English and Tourism, proved to be an expert guide. He showed us all sorts of local flora and fauna we never would have seen on our own. We learned that the *Madroño* is the national tree of Nicaragua. Yader showed us the *dormilona*, a beautiful, tiny fern that folds into itself the instant you (or Harlan or Olle) touch it, setting off giggles and oohs and aahs every time. Yader and Adilsa also showed us the *jaboncillo* tree, whose leaves were used as a natural scrubber of dirty dishes all over rural Nicaragua up until the arrival of the common, synthetic sponge to the region only some fifteen years ago in many places.

It's funny sometimes, when perspective turns the commonplace into the extraordinary. Our hike up Rota included several unusual sightings, such as two parrot-like birds in the jungle canopy above us and a nut called the *Ojo de Buey* (Bull's eye), a smooth, round fruit that not only can burn your skin when rubbed vociferously against a rock (cue Yader's burnt arm) but is also used to make necklaces and wooden pegs for chairs. Less exotic for us, but clearly a rare occurrence for our local guides, was the unmistakable leaf shaking that is only produced by the common *ardilla* (squirrel). Coming from the squirrel metropolis that is the Northeast US, we found ourselves in unfamiliar territory, running, tripping, and clamoring to catch sight of and maintain the energy and excitement being expressed by both Yader and Adilsa at not one but two *ardillas* jumping from branch to branch. But what a great lesson, that we can and should find ways to experience newness in the mundane, joy in what might seem like the ordinary.

The hike up Rota introduced us to an even deeper level of poverty then exists in most of El Tololar. At the top we came upon a building that serves as the kindergarten through 6th grade school for 27 students. It is extremely basic, and we found that the rustic desks arrived there on the backs of six or eight volunteers who huffed them up the side of the mountain about four years ago. We met the current teacher, a man of about 30 years old, on his way down to a spring, the only local water source, about a ¼ mile down a steep hill from the school. It was a Saturday but all the students were there, neatly dressed and waiting for staff from the non-governmental organization (NGO) World Vision to arrive with certificates of completion for school and a piñata. The few houses and huts that surround the school have no electricity, and only arduous access to water.

As with many parts of the world, it is a really tough life, even if surrounded by beauty. Hiking past the simple houses reminded us of a mantra we adopted as a family when providing financial support for our friend Ivania to buy a horse: hotel or horse, horse or hotel. For the price of a one night's stay in a mid-range hotel in the States, you can buy a horse here in Nicaragua. A pretty powerful reminder that proves the equation:

Small investments + small sacrifices = BIG DIFFERENCE.

Most of us at one time or another have experienced the triumphant prize that is the dead mouse your cat lays at your feet or on your doorstep after a successful hunt. The cat is very proud, and at the same time, you are very grossed out. We've experienced this multiple times here in Nicaragua, but with a lizard serving as the cat's trophy. Usually Dulce just finds small lizards about 3 inches long and plays with them (or tortures, depending on your point of view) on our patio, at times letting the crippled little gal or guy slither back into one of our rooms, only to be found later. Last week, Dulce's prize was the hindquarters of a rather larger lizard, set neatly next to our refrigerator and drying nicely in the afternoon sun that shone through our wood-framed window. Hard to get used to for sure, but likely a small price to pay in exchange for not only the lizards but all the crickets Dulce eats and the mice she keeps at bay.

Wednesday was *Dia de los Difuntos* here in El Tololar and all across Nicaragua. Despite the rather morbid name, translated "Day of the Deceased", it is a notable holiday that literally brings the whole country together. It actually starts three or four days before in marketplaces, side streets, roadside stalls and supermarkets. We first experienced it when our bus dropped us off at the edge of the bus terminal in León. The usual fruit sellers, money-changers, hardware shops, and food stalls were barely noticeable. The entire marketplace had exploded with reds, yellows, greens, violets…

every color imaginable, embodied in beautiful flowers and "snow" (tiny, round pieces of dyed Styrofoam) being sold in every nook and what seemed like new crannies that had been built just for the occasion. Over the following days these rainbows would be bought in large quantities and brought to cemeteries to adorn the graves of loved ones.

We had the opportunity to walk to the graveyard in El Tololar with Adilsa and her granddaughter Rachel. There we spent an hour or more laying flowers and sprinkling snow on several of the hundreds of graves there (Adilsa's grandparents, uncles and aunts, and a nephew who had died way too young were all buried in close proximity). Family upon family came and went all day, remembering the dead and at the same time, connecting with the living. Food sellers were omnipresent with *buñuelos* (delicious, fried balls of yucca and sugar and topped with honey) serving as the traditional treat. It was a festive environment, accentuated by smiles, bright colors, and fond memories. Being the only real resident gringos in town, we were clearly outsiders but were welcomed into the moment with open arms.

A week or so ago, Don Leonel's horse arrived for a morning grazing session near our house with a purple-painted back and some rather nasty wounds. The injury could have come from almost anything, and we thought it was likely from a barbed-wire fence crossing gone wrong. Bats *(murciélagos)* weren't our first suspicion. It turns out that in addition to scorpions, tarantulas, biting ants, flies, gnats and termites, we need to add bats – check that, vampire bats – to our list of flying/biting animals that we don't really like. For Don Leonel, the phrase – in Spanish – "Oh yes, that purple stuff on my horse's back is just iodine and medicine to treat the wound from the vampire bat that was sucking his neck a few nights back" seemed to roll of his tongue with the greatest of ease, as if he'd just been asked about the weather. Our reaction, on the other hand, was somewhat more animated, and included phrases like, "holy sh_! A vampire bat sucked your horse's neck?"

Approximately one third of our lives here are spent under mosquito nets while we sleep. The funny thing is that so far, there really have not been that many mosquitoes. But during dark, rainy, thunderstorm filled nights it sure can feel good to be protected, if even by a hyper-thin material, from the creepy-crawlies that you know are lurking nearby. The nets came in particularly handy not three nights past after Miriam and Cully had spotted our seventh or eighth tarantula near the top corner of the wall that separates our room from the boy's room. Cully's initial whack attempt with Miriam's sandal was a blatant miss. This meant one of two things; the tarantula had either scurried over one wall and outside, or over the other wall and into the boy's room. Fortunately, a thorough search of the Harlan and Olle's room uncovered nothing, while a second whack on our back wall with a sneaker while balancing precariously on our crooked eating table hit the mark.

Learning a new language is always tough, and Spanish is no exception. One of the great things, though, is that many words are cognates with English, with very similar spelling and meaning, yet vastly different pronunciation. Take *temperatura*, *locomoción*, and *domesticar*. They all basically mean what they sound like. But often words in Spanish have very different meanings and are only off by a letter or two. For example: *verde* (green) and *verdad* (truth). Several times, when attempting to reinforce a statement, we declared, "Ain't that the green!" Or *rato* (a while) and *raton* (mouse). The phrase, "For goodness' sake, can you just wait a mouse!" or something similar may have been uttered a time or two by one or several Lundgrens. But often it's not the Spanish but the English phrases we'll remember. Olle summed up a recent walk near the bus station with the apt description, "It smells like wet poop." It kind of did.

Small investments + small sacrifices = BIG DIFFERENCE

Soon we hope to tell you more stories that prove this equation. These kinds of stories are growing here. It can at times be frustrating for us because things just take more time in Nicaragua. We want to make a difference immediately, change lives now, instantly. But we need to have patience, and so we wait, and plan for tomorrow. In the meantime, we take baby steps. This afternoon we will go with our friend to a nearby school and play with the children, teaching English while learning Spanish, always it seems, receiving more than we can ever give.

Chapter 8:
Singing Karaoke, Owls, Frozen Termites

Mid-November

To give an insight into the mind of an eleven year-old, Harlan gave us permission to include a couple short excerpts from his diary since we've been here:

> "The days are slowly blowing together, but it feels so slow. It feels like we're two months in but we haven't even been here for a month. As each day goes by I miss people more and more. To think they are doing the first year of Middle School without me…"
>
> "I stand in the middle of a field and look up and say the clouds and the sky look similar in the United States. I have so many reminders of the United States; everything. Sometimes it's good and sometimes it's bad."
>
> "I could write for a hundred years just to give you a taste of what I am thinking and feeling, and how hard it is to be here, but the bottom line is I really want to be home."
>
> "We go to the city once a week. It is short but it is like a small, 5-hour break from El Tololar. Sometimes we have a special

> American meal too, but we always have to go back to El Tololar. It is fun."
>
> "Costa Rica vacation is coming up soon. It is going to be fun but the problem is waiting to get there. I hate weekends here. I know it sounds weird but there is nothing to do on weekends, nothing."

People and places are like onions and icebergs, always much deeper and more layered when you dig, dive and peel into lives. A recent conversation with our friend Wilmar provided one such onion-iceberg moment. Previously, we told about the social and economic challenges that are the reality for smallholder farming communities like El Tololar. But there is a much larger macro-economic story going on in places like Nicaragua and our little village that has a human face, and goes by many names like Nestor, Oscar, Paula, Franklin and Fernando. This story is very personal, and it impacts just about everyone who lives here. It's kind of like a mosquito, sucking life instead of giving it, conveying viruses instead of opportunities. Every story is a little different, but allow us to share one from Wilmar's perspective. He's twenty-nine years old, and his collective experience is as illustrative as any, a mix of dashed dreams, loss, happiness and contentment, possibilities blocked by the realities of life here, complacency and perseverance, always perseverance.

The winding conversation with Wilmar, on his front stoop but underneath one of the three types of lemon trees in his yard, began with him sharing his desire to start a small computer repair shop. Wilmar actually went to college and studied law for several years but had to drop out when he ran out of money. During that time he was married to Mariella, had a beautiful daughter named Rachel, and lost a son during childbirth. He currently lives in a home on the family property near our house. Mariella works in Managua (a minimum 3-hour commute away) seven days a week, twelve to fourteen hours a day at a giant retail store. She gets paid very little, but it's a job. Normally, Mariella and Rachel are in Managua for two-week stretches and then come here to El Tololar every other weekend. It's a tough life for their little family.

If the economics of life here were different, it's possible that Wilmar, like other young men in the *campo* (countryside), would have become a farmer. And had he come of age a few decades earlier, he might have been able to make a real go of it. At that time, current President Daniel Ortega (re-elected two days before the 2016 US elections in a landslide victory that was hailed locally as being free and fair – cue the huge wink, wink here) had just come to power as the head of the Sandinistas, who many readers will recall in connection with names like Oliver North, Iran, and Contras. In short, during the 1980s the US used funds from the sale of arms to Iran to secretly funnel money to the Contra Rebels, fighting against Ortega's Sandinistas. Like other socialist movements across Latin America and the world, the US feared a domino-effect of leaders like Ortega and Castro coming to power and took great efforts to support opposing rebel groups like the Contras.

If you were a young man like Wilmar living in a rural Nicaraguan village in the 1980s, though, Ortega and the Sandinistas symbolized hope. They had overthrown the previous brutal dictatorship of the Somoza family, which lasted from 1937-1979. According to Wilmar, in the early years the Sandinistas delivered on their promises, providing land, tools and economic opportunities to impoverished rural families. But the party didn't last long, and Ortega and others soon began taking for themselves what they had promised to give to the people. Back to the wink-wink from above, despite Ortega's recent "landslide" victory with some 72% of the vote and purportedly legitimized by international observers, few people in El Tololar, if speaking on condition of anonymity, would have anything good to say about the current government.

For Wilmar and others, there have been moments of hope, times when things were looking up. Like the time several years back when Elio, our new Cuban friend who married a local woman, tried to start a local producer group of farmers who could use strength in numbers to buy a tractor and obtain bank investment. But because the bank would only provide a loan with a 24% interest rate at best, they lost money and ended up worse off than before. Another time they had a bumper crop of yucca, one of the best ever. But so did many others, and the market price was so low that they couldn't make any profit. Compounding the challenges were basic things like transportation: their land was far away and they couldn't afford to buy or even rent a truck to haul the yucca to market. And they didn't have a tractor. Economies everywhere and anywhere need to have at least a few key elements in place in order to foster real opportunity: supportive government, access to investment, suitable infrastructure for moving goods, technological advancement, realistic tax rates, etc. The proper mix and inputs depends on your perspective and personal ideology, but with Nicaragua remaining the second poorest country in the Western Hemisphere, clearly something is not going right.

So what happens when there is no economic opportunity in a place like Nicaragua? Young people do one of four things:

1. They continue to try and farm, even when the deck is increasingly stacked against them.
2. They leave their families and move to another country like Costa Rica or Guatemala (moving to the US is the gold standard but beyond most people's imagination) searching for employment.
3. They join the military, a hard life to be sure but providing some sense of security, for a time.
4. They get a job with one of the big, local international companies like Yazaki. Some 10,000 people in the area work for Yazaki alone, a global automotive parts supplier. There they work long hours for little pay, and usually only because they feel it is their only option.

The fifth alternative is to have a little imagination, some skills and a little training (Wilmar has taken a computer repair class and is really good at fixing things), a bit of fortune, and a little outside help. Then you can consider starting a computer repair shop, like Wilmar. He dreams of using his hands to fix hard drives, motherboards, and microchips. He dreams of living together with his wife and daughter, and investing in his entire extended family with the profit from his business. One of our projects here in El Tololar is to support Wilmar's dream with an initial investment to help him get going, one computer at a time.

Colds, diseases and injuries are always a bummer. Here they take on a new meaning because it seems like in the eleven weeks since we've arrived, one or more of us, at one time or another, have been sick or injured. The few moments of sobriety from sickness have been filled with other discomforts, not huge inconveniences but big enough to make you say, "You've got to be kidding me!"

Exhaustive sickness and injury list to date: diarrhea (of course), general stomach pains, vomiting, fevers, sore throats, eye and ear infections, bruised ribs, twisted knees, strange rashes, assorted cuts, scrapes and bites, migraine headaches, and bouts of constipation.

List of uncomfortable things that are tolerable on some days but can put you over the edge on others: creepy crawlies, never-ending gnats, flies on food, tarantulas in room, shower scorpions, biting ants (literally, it is hard to have a conversation, not on concrete, brick or tile, that doesn't include at least one of the participants lifting their leg, dancing or swatting wildly, and saying something like "ahh, yah, ouch, damn, or during the all-too common multiple bite sessions, you little sh_"), multi-day power outages and the ensuing sour frijoles or pineapple, no running water for days at a time, volcanic-soil charged thunder and lightning storms, more dirt five minutes after you've swept, semi-feral dogs attempting to eat your rabbit, poopy rain, rainy poop, cockroaches in latrines at night, and going to bed smelly due to having no water.

On the fifth of November, the weather changed. Political pundits in the US would say it changed on November 8th, the day Donald Trump was elected, but here in El Tololar, it changed on the morning of November 5th. We arrived during the rainy season and our first two months were mostly about rain. People told us that the official winter (*invierno*) would end in early November and we would enter six months of the dry season, summer (*verano*).

There is a scene in the movie Mary Poppins where the weather changes in a moment, the weathervane on the top of the captain's house shifts 180 degrees and a new season starts.

In El Tololar, on November 5th, we woke and it was cool. It was dry. It was summer. We may not see a rain drop again until May.

Our whole family took a walk last week with our neighbor Adilsa to her school. She is the librarian, and also one of the school administrators. She is also a truly amazing person. She introduced us to each class, most kids giggling and quite fascinated, especially with Harlan and Olle. We were a bit confused when several third-grade students, when asked where they thought we were from, indicated Spain. Clearly there was something missing as even on our best language day, we could never double as Spaniards. Being at the school felt really fulfilling. Harlan and Olle met a lot of kids their age, and had a chance to play kickball with their new friends. Miriam and Cully spent time helping Adilsa categorize books, assigning a number to each, kind of Dewey-Decimal style.

Summer break starts soon here, and our goal until then is to go to the school once or twice a week and resume again after vacation. Harlan and Olle will attend school those days, and Cully and Miriam will teach English. Those of us who are native English speakers often take for granted the gift we've been given, just to know the language. When we asked the sixth grade class for a show of hands of who wanted to learn English, every single hand shot up. We look forward to sharing this gift in El Tololar in the coming months.

During a rainstorm, never hold an important meeting when the following elements are present:

1. a tin roof
2. a relatively unfamiliar language

3. a local guy with a particularly strong accent that is exceptionally hard to understand.

The combination above, we found out, can result in the head of a local agriculture cooperative leaving a meeting with the strong feeling that in the near future you will both be assisting him to get a visa to the US while personally financing his one-million dollar yucca processing manufacturing plant endeavor. It is now our job to attempt to clarify our actual intent to the cooperative's president, conveying the notion that our collective nods of approval were meant to impart understanding and a listening ear, not that the Lundgren family would forevermore be the cooperative's benefactors, as much as we would like to if we could.

"Honey, should I take the termites out of the freezer so they can thaw?" This was the question Cully posed to Miriam one night, just before bedtime. The seed for the query was planted earlier in the day by a fifth-grade student named Grainer. Grainer had interrupted a lively conversation taking place in the school library. He was followed closely by four friends, one of whom was carrying a partially maimed but still rambunctious owl.

Grainer began gesticulating loudly and explaining that he had come across the owl (*cocoroca)* earlier in the morning in a field near his house. His assessment was that it had been hit by a slingshot and judging by the owl's one-eye scowl and inability to open his mouth, a rock to the face was indeed a solid appraisal of his current status. Adilsa managed to coax the owl first onto her shoulder (and away from five screaming boys who were tormenting the poor little gal) and subsequently onto Miriam's. Olle, who loves animals and is really the reason we now have a cat, rabbit and an Owl, offered his shoulder as another option and there Ow-ey (a nickname bestowed by Olle) remained for the rest of the morning. We soon came to understand that in fact Ow-ey was a gift from Grainer, who seemed grateful to be relieved of the responsibility of trying to feed a partially blind, reticent to eat owl.

We took the dirt road home, calculating it would have fewer barking dogs on it, with Ow-ey on Olle's shoulder, hiding her head from the noon sun under his sombrero while intermittently digging her talons into his skin in order to keep from falling off in her weakened state. We arrived home and headed straight to the nearest *venta*, as we had received a tip that the proprietor's daughter was a veterinarian in training. Taking a shortcut to avoid two large bulls that were yoked together and standing in the middle of the road – their opposing movements ensuring they remained smack in the middle with no room to pass – we arrived at the store to find that the daughter was not home but that we could try back later. We returned home at a bit of a loss as to what our plan of attack should be and were lucky to find that our friend Marden had just stopped by to say hi.

Marden works as a tour guide, often taking guests up the nearby Cerro Negro (translated "Black Hill" in English) to surf down on homemade sand boards, and is very handy with exotic and wild animals. We knew this because Marden had previously shown us pictures of him posing with snakes, monkeys, and anteaters he had come across. Marden immediately took over, diagnosing the owl, cleaning out the wound on her beak and disinfecting her bad eye, which by now was covered in hundreds of gnats. It was when the question of food came up that things got interesting for some, and downright gross for others.

Ow-ey could barely open her mouth and with only one good eye we knew she wasn't yet ready to hunt. Marden suggested termites, and Adilsa seemed sure that *gusanos* (worms) would do the trick. Upon request, Wilmar was more than happy to share his termite (locally known as *comején*) mound with us. Marden cracked off the top, revealing thousands of white squirmy guys, which he assured us did not bite, proving it by eating five or six himself. We captured a small bowl full, the hundreds that spilled being quickly eaten by 10 or 15 nearby chickens. We found a few worms in the ears of corn Don Leonel picked for us, and were ready to go. Our new ritual, roughly four times a day until Ow-ey improves enough to be set free, involves Miriam holding Ow-ey (as she digs her claws into her hand) while Cully carefully places partially-thawed termites in her mouth, washing them down with a splash of water. "Yes, honey, please thaw the termites…"

Corn is being cut across Nicaragua, and that means that the stalks near our home will soon come down, changing the vista from our front patio substantially. It will no longer have that *ear-y* feel, but again, as when we first arrived here and the corn was still nascent, Don Leonel's horses will come into view where the corn once stood. We will be able to see Esteban's house, along with cows, bulls, chickens and dogs, through the eucalyptus trees. We will also eat a lot, we mean a lot, of corn.

Miriam had the chance last week to take part in an eleven-step process that is an annual event in homes across Nicaragua—making *tamales dulce* (sweet tamales). Tamale-making includes, among other steps, picking the *elotes* (fresh ears of corn), dehusking then cutting the kernels off, grinding into a paste and adding sugar, cinnamon, and local cheese for the special sweet sauce, mixing the rest of the paste and wrapping inside the corn husks, boiling in the fire for an hour… and eating. Delicious, but because these specific tamales can only be made with corn when it is soft and young, they come hot and heavy for a time. We've eaten a lot in the past week or so, a new sweet treat, made by different neighbors, arriving at our doorstep daily and sometimes hourly.

Sweet tamales are not the only syrupy treat here in Nicaragua. Some days we find ourselves reaching a point of sweetness overload, at least such was the case last week. We had *nacatamales* for breakfast (not sweet but really rich). These were followed up by successive servings of *tamales dulce*, delivered in quick succession first by Paula and then Adilsa. Not long after, we were served sweet, homemade fruit juice at the home of our friend Ivania: ice-cold and delicious, but very sugary. On our walk home, we ran into Fernando and Jessica, whose mother whipped up a fresh batch of *banana con leche* – another delectable drink but again, really sweet. We were so grateful for the hospitality and generosity, but by that point we were done, kaput, and shut-off. In front of us, with bellies full, we had to be our best for the weekly Sunday afternoon soccer game at Don Leonel's, which has become quite an affair. Amazingly, despite the sugar high, or possibly because of it, we all played pretty well, a relative term as some of the local, barefoot soccer players are legit amazing!

Last Friday, through a series of events, Miriam, Cully, Harlan and Olle found themselves at the front of the auditorium at *Lechecuagos* Secondary School, preparing to judge the school's first ever English Karaoke singing contest, along with a local judge named Carlos. *Lechecuagos'* English teacher, Isidro, was understandably nervous with all the things that could go wrong, but ended up fulfilling his MC duties perfectly and with panache. The competition's five song entries included "My Heart Will Go On", by Celine Dion and "Baby Can I Hold You Tonight", by Tracy Chapman. For a time the front-runner was a handsome young man named Erbil who performed a cracking, acoustic version of "Wake Me Up When September Ends" by Green Day. And Erbil would have won, had it not been for two previously unknown entrants who hit the ball out of the park with a stomping, crowd-pleasing rendition of "The Judge", by the Ohio-based band Twenty-One Pilots. It was agreed by all, including our fellow-judge Carlos, that indeed "The Judge" was the best and the two singers were over the moon to have won. We all had a blast serving as judges. Plus, the street cred we achieved simply by being native English speakers helped offset the discomfort we collectively felt from having to make mini-speeches in Spanish to 500 students.

Once recent morning, we walked as a family to the local health clinic in El Tololar. It's about a 20-minute walk through three peanut fields to the small rectangular turquoise building that serves as the main health post for all of El Tololar as well as several surrounding communities. Surely there are health posts that make do with less, but as assuredly there are others that are equipped with a lot more.

The examination room is very simple, with ripped vinyl beds, a coat rack, and a couple old stethoscopes hanging on the wall. El Tololar's clinic ostensibly receives medical supply donations from the government but the deliveries are very sporadic, and often sorely lacking in content. After a short tour, for example, we were ushered in to speak with the head doctor, Maria. She told us that they had received several diabetes glucometers recently but that they had arrived without the strips required to do the glucose check. Strips are expensive, and they don't have the money to purchase them. So the meters sit and gather dust. Maria also told us that they would like to get a computer to log data accurately, and that other needs included soap, scissors, and surgical masks. Plus basic things, like fans and chairs. A generous friend has said he would donate the $400 necessary to cover the basics. As we left the clinic and walked home, Olle said, "It feels good to be helping." And it does.

The first two and one-half months in Nicaragua have allowed us to laugh, cry, scream, be euphoric, depressed, stink, care for others, experience giving, love and be loved, rely on faith, family and friends, and search for meaning. It is impacting each one of us differently, and it has been hard, perhaps even harder than we thought; the homesickness can be the hardest. The whole adventure has and always will be framed through a daily lens of rice and beans. Life here is not easy, and we hope that the experience is providing us even a taste, a glimmer of how hard life is not only in El Tololar, Nicaragua, but in Honduras, Mexico, Syria, Sudan, and in places closer to home like countless inner-city or rural, poverty-stricken communities across the US.

Chapter 9:
Super-Hyper-Mega-Ultra-Gigantisimo, Cockroach Sipping

Late November/ Early December

Kids do and say the darndest things. Last week, Olle came back to the house before Harlan after a session of tag and general roughhousing with their friend Leo. Very nonchalantly, Olle quipped, "Harlan and Leo were playing with their fists. A few seconds ago they were using machetes, but they stopped." Well, that's a relief!

December 1st, and another Lundgren is down and out. Olle was a beast on the soccer field as recently as yesterday, running around like a madman with his red shorts and black headband. Shirtless, he took on any and every opponent as he weaved in between the coconut trees, dodging fallen grapefruit while getting covered with the telltale volcanic dust that is the soil of El Tololar. Today he woke up with a fever, and has fought it all day. We are at 101 plus right now, at times flirting with 102 under the arm, and may need to take him in to the doctor by motorcycle soon.

We have attempted on several occasions to burn our garbage. In general, it has been a complete fail. This is mostly because we only dug one hole for our garbage and we mix paper, plastic and organic together. The hole sits in our backyard, shaded by several trees that line Don Leonel's adjacent bean field. It gets some sun, but even if it baked all day for several days, banana peels, grapefruit husks, leftover pineapple, and watermelon rinds just don't burn very well. Next time we need to dig a hole, we will dig two and practice proper organic separation!

Burning weeds is a different story though. Carlo has cut our weeds twice now, and each time we have been left with a giant pile of assorted cuttings. The first time we tried to burn them was during the rainy season and it just wouldn't catch fire (we haven't come across any good lighter fluid). Last week we tried again, Miriam and Cully lighting whatever dry egg cartons, boxes and paper products we could find. The fire started with a roar and for a moment we were feeling quite proud, particularly because we had fortunately chosen a day with little wind and thus were not smoking out our neighbors. The weeds on top were dry enough but deep down it was wet. We each danced around the fire for the better part of an hour, a strange looking ritual for any passersby for sure, us prodding, poking and circling the pile together, rhythmically, in an attempt to keep the flame lit. Ultimately the wind shifted toward our house, and we were left with a smoldering pile of weeds and smoke in our faces. The best part was that the fire did actually continue, smoking and smoldering for two days, and finally did succeed in burning all our weeds.

Full disclosure: We have a pee bucket. This is not something you normally divulge, but we really feel a kinship with all our readers and are ready to share the truth with you. Okay, we didn't start with a pee bucket. At first we made the journey to either Wilmar or our neighbor Miriam's latrine for both #1 and #2. But one day Miriam had the genius idea that the green garbage can in our room was only being lightly used for rubbish and that it could easily transform into a pee bucket. A pee bucket would allow all urination to occur in-house, saving us multiple day and night time privy walks and avoiding encounters with the array of spooky creatures residing in and around the latrine.

The pee bucket is now used by all four Lundgren family members throughout the day (it remains our little secret) and is dumped each morning into our garbage hole, another reason why it refuses to burn. We keep a supply of bleach handy to disinfect and have a strict #1 only policy that has only been broken once, during an intestinal emergency. In general we can highly recommend the pee bucket, and now it only seems a bit out of place when one of us needs to urinate during the boys' school hours. "Hi Harlan," Cully might say as he uses the container placed in the corner of our bedroom/classroom. "What have you learned today in social studies? Oh interesting, I had forgotten that the Paleolithic Age lasted up until 8,000 B.C. Bye for now…"

Miriam and Cully may in fact have one of the most uncomfortable beds of all time, although the type we use is commonplace throughout El Tololar. Harlan and Olle sleep on 'scissor beds' that are basically a bag used to hold rice and beans pulled tightly across a simple wooden frame. They have largely positive reviews of the beds' comfort. The double bed in Miriam and Cully's room looks restful enough. It has two thin mattresses (we bought an extra one soon after we arrived to augment) and appears inviting. It has a simple wood frame and a wicker (*junco*) base with no cross-beam supports. Herein seems to lie the problem. Generally, soon after we have dozed off, Miriam 'rolls' downhill toward Cully, coming to a rest almost on top of him. We then spend the rest of the night on the flat half of the bed, snug for sure, but not as spacious as desired. We have taken great pains to identify the source of the slope, but it continues to elude us, even after going underneath the bed to inspect, like a mechanic checking the brakes. The incline – or decline depending on the sleeper's perspective – remains a mystery.

Our owl died just before we left for our Costa Rican vacation. We had Ow-ey for the better part of six days. We fed her tens of termites and at least thirty or forty worms we found in rotting husks in the nearby cornfield. We used our fingers to dip water in her mouth. We pet her and endured cuts from her talons. She put up the good fight but went downhill quickly late last Monday night. First she wouldn't even keep a worm down, then her foot cramped up and she couldn't hold on to her roost. Finally she couldn't even stand, and we watched her die as she lay on her side in the hutch we bought for our rabbit Rainer. Losing Ow-ey was a real downer as we had all grown fond of her and admired her determination to live despite the odds being stacked against her; RIP Ow-ey.

It took us exactly six local bus changes and one taxi ride to cross the border and reach the beach in Samara, Costa Rica, a brief but much anticipated vacation. We ended up leaving a day early due to news of the impending Otto, a very rare, late season hurricane that came on shore as a category two storm in eastern Nicaragua on Thanksgiving Day. It took us an extra day to reach our destination as we were forced to hole-up in the lovely Casa San Juan Hostel in Managua for a night. This delay was the result of Harlan's rapidly deteriorating stomach trouble, made worse by an excessively greasy but tasty enchilada we purchased after our first bus ride. By the time we reached the hotel, not only had Harlan's stomach problems reached a crisis point, but Miriam's pants had been ruined by the grease that seeped out of the suspect enchilada.

At Casa San Juan we were introduced to the thrilling 'suicide shower' (we learned the name later from a couple we met in Costa Rica), evidently not a hard apparatus to find in parts of Central America. The ingenious invention (which allows hostels to advertise that they offer hot showers) has a valve attached to the nozzle with three settings: hot, warm and cold. Coming into the valve are three different color electrical filaments. The shower must get its euphemistic name either from these dangerous looking wires (water with wires nearby always presents a scary situation) or from the 'hot' setting. In fact, it should read "scalding, don't use this setting in isolation or you may die."

It turns out the only way to successfully use a suicide shower is by deploying the buddy system. One person showers per usual, the other stands at attention above, ready to change the setting whenever the person showering says, "switch!" In this way it is possible to take a shower that stays mostly in the lukewarm range with only brief moments of wicked hot or freezing cold.

Unwittingly, Miriam nearly ingested a cockroach one recent evening. We had just returned from Costa Rica to a home with no electricity and no running water. We had stocked up our giant 5-gallon water containers weeks before which was great, but as the water had been stagnant for a while we decided it was best to use the *LifeStraws* Miriam's parents had purchased for us before we came. These straws, by the way, are amazing and allow you to sip water even from a dirty puddle if the need presents itself. Miriam took a well-deserved straw swig, followed shortly thereafter by screams and a confused cockroach running for dear life. Lesson learned? Always close *LifeStraw* lid when not using for an extended period of time.

In Nicaragua, at least, banana plants have magical powers. They attract poisonous animals, and at the same time make them disappear. And everyone here seems to know it. For example, upon finding a scorpion in our kitchen, our friend Beto trapped it and directly carried it over and slid it down into the banana plant. Our friend Marden was over at our house not long after. He saw Cully pick up a small, red, ant looking insect. He told us it was poisonous, at which point Cully said, "So we should kill it right?" Marden said yes, but then proceeded, like Beto, to slide the insect (still alive) down into the nearby banana plant. We continue to wonder what is really down in between those leaves and what makes it such a good repository for arthropods…

In cross-cultural settings, you often find yourself doing or seeing things that are either just weird, or plain funny. We recently took a bus ride with friends to a nearby hot springs. Prior to a bus switch, Cully looked out the window and said to Olle, "Hey, look at that guy caring that giant piece of meat." Upon closer examination, the meat was actually a massive pig head, just going for a morning stroll with his owner. Olle's eyes got pretty huge. Another time, Harlan and Cully were looking to purchase ibuprofen. The only stuff available stated explicitly that it was for menstrual cramps. But 200mg of ibuprofen is 200mg of ibuprofen, we surmised, and we hoped it worked equally well for all of us!

In Spanish, at least in Nicaraguan Spanish, they often use either diminutives (Harlan and Olle for example are not *gringos* but *gringitos*, our kitten is not a gata but a gatita). It's kind of cool because you can add 'ita', or 'ito' to lots of words to convey a sense of connection or cuteness. The same goes for extra-sizing things. In the USA you might go to McDonalds and 'Super-Size' your order. In Nicaragua, they take it even a step further, as we found out on our trip to Costa Rica, driving by a giant sign stating that the upcoming sale was sure to be 'Super-Hyper-Mega-Ultra-Gigantisimo' in nature. Beat that!

What does it take to be an angel in Nicaragua? Not that much, really just a small donation to make a big impact. In the world of finance, an "Angel Investor" is someone (or a group of people) who provide much needed financial capital, usually to start-up companies. They are angels to the people who run the companies because often they are the only ones willing to take a risk on a great idea, on a dream. They make a potentially risky investment, and take a leap of faith.

During a conversation with our friends, Wilmar and Adilsa, around Adilsa's kitchen table a few nights back, we had what might be categorized as an epiphany. It went (and goes) something like this. We are already Angel Investors, or perhaps a better moniker is Micro-Angel investors. We have some disposable capital, and before us we have people, the people of El Tololar. These people have big dreams. We have an opportunity now to invest in these dreams. Many people have done this through support of our family. If you want to do more for the awesome, inspiring people of El Tololar, you can make a donation directly online to the work of our partner organization, Tololamos, at www.tololamos.org.

Chapter 10:
Volcano Surfing, Screaming for Candy, Ain't No BULL!

Mid-December

Her name means "brilliant star", and her future is now brighter. Last week we had the opportunity to meet Slilma, the first of two university students who will be receiving one of the seven scholarships we are helping to provide. Each applicant went through a vetting process administered by Tololamos, and ultimately the final candidates were chosen based on grades and conduct; students in particularly tough economic situations were prioritized. We sat in a circle on the dirt patio outside Adilsa's kitchen. Adilsa and Wilmar represented Tololamos. Miriam and Cully (and later Harlan) represented "Familia Lundgren." Slilma sat cross-legged on a rickety plastic chair, at first slightly disengaged, in between her father, Paulo, and her mother, Beliza.

Slilma is sixteen years old (students often complete secondary school here at that age) and hopes to study nursing and/or accounting at a public university in León. Her family is poor and does not have the means to send her to school. Mid-way through our meeting, Paulo took his hat off, revealing a partially-caved in skull on the left side of his head, the result of a serious bike accident while riding home from work early one morning last year. He can't work now and receives very little in the way of disability. Beliza doesn't have a job and spends her time caring for the family. They understand the value of education on a deep level, Paulo noting that "Every boy or girl who doesn't have an education has no future."

Adilsa read the scholarship requirements (maintain a good grade point average, treat others respectfully, no drugs, etc.) then presented Slilma with $80 cash, a part of the scholarship used to help her buy books and prepare for school. When the new school year starts, Slilma will receive $40/month for 10 months of school each year (as long as she adheres to the scholarships requisites). The scholarship will continue until she finishes, which could be five years. One year seems an inadequate amount of time to support a dream. Slilma and her parents smiled with gratitude as they left, and so did we.

Florinda the chicken has a funny habit. She lays exactly one egg almost every day at about 11:30 a.m., just before lunch. She lays the egg smack in the middle of our 10-year-old neighbor Leo's bed, cackling proudly, at which point Leo retrieves the egg and places it in the kitchen while Florinda walks outside with her friends. We think Florinda is also in the same posse of chickens that make a beeline for our house every morning when they are let out of their hutch by Adilsa at about 5:20 a.m., circling our patio in search of the last night's dinner scraps while Miriam and Cully exercise to greet the day.

Another gang of chickens, residing at Miriam and Carlos's, also frequent our home, at times even having the moxie to enter our kitchen. When our neighbor Miriam calls them with a "coouuueeeee" each evening, they cluck and flap home excitedly with astonishing speed. Upon eating a traditional meal of chicken, bananas, rice and vegetables that Miriam recently prepared for us, however, we came to find out that their fervor to get home to roost is at times imprudent as her call can signify food or imminent death.

We have a two-foot high plastic Christmas tree, bought in the crowded León market near the lady from whom we buy our beans and rice. The tree is heavily laden with many of the hand-made *jicaro* ornaments our friend Fernando made for us. Olle made a paper star that sits atop. Fernando and his brother Yader brought the bulbs to our house recently, along with a bag of hand-picked roasted peanuts that we ate for a week while contemplating the local and global implications of the peanut industry.

On a previous visit to their house, Yader had shared with us a video of a scorpion he had found under a piece of wood. He and Fernando, 19 and 18 respectively, mentioned that they couldn't even count the number of times they had each been stung, but that it was *bastante* (which basically means a lot). Our obvious interest in Yader's scorpion must have led him to the erroneous conclusion that we in fact like having scorpions around, and along with the Christmas bulbs and peanuts, Yader brought a jar holding a giant scorpion he had caught. He kept saying, "don't worry don't worry," while periodically taking the creature out on the concrete floor near our kitchen and prodding it with a stick. Miriam did a great job in showing culturally sensitive restraint – perhaps being gifted a scorpion was in fact a great honor – by adopting only her 'polite' shriek technique in the hopes that Yader would eventually take the hint that we already had enough pets, which he finally did.

We've averaged about a scorpion and a tarantula every two weeks. Not bad. The tarantula count went up last weekend when we had successive sightings (and subsequent killings) about 12 hours apart. The first tarantula, whom our cat Dulce had already partially incapacitated, met its demise on the bottom of Cully's flip-flop, just outside our kitchen. The second sighting began innocently enough with Miriam washing clothes last Saturday morning. Upon picking up a particularly crusty pair of Harlan's shorts, she felt something slither up her arm. It wasn't huge, but for goodness' sakes, it was a freakin' tarantula! We all came running, and our neighbor Aquiles found two sticks and picked it up from amidst the clothes, chopstick style. He placed it on the ground nearby. Aquiles was clearly on the tarantula's side as he, like Yader, kept saying "no problem, no worries," his way of advocating strongly for saving its life. It's wonderful that people here are connected to nature. They live so close to a wide variety of animals that everything, even scary spiders, are just a part of living here. But in the end the "Hey man, I just had a tarantula on my arm while washing clothes and I'm just a little freaked" argument won out, and Aquiles pushed her into the ground with a pointy stick.

After three months, we finally went volcano boarding. In fact volcano boarding can only be done in a few places on earth, one of which is on the side of Cerro Negro, an active volcano 30 minutes from our house by motorcycle. Cerro Negro only came into being in 1850 and thus holds the distinction of being the youngest active volcano on earth. It is actually a beautiful mountain, about 700 meters high, that grows a few meters each year (or more during an eruption year, of which there have been about 28 since its birth). Its blackness is beautiful in stark contrast to the verdant green, dormant volcanoes and fields that surround it.

Boarding or 'surfing' the mountain requires that you rent a *tabla* (a basic wooden snowboard looking contraption without the straps), carry it up the mountain (or carry yours and your kids) and then choose one of several trails to slide down. It's wise to wear long pants and sleeves, goggles, gloves and even a whole bright orange or yellow jumpsuit you are provided if you go with a local tour company. You sit on the board like a sled (you can try standing but word is that it's exceedingly difficult), and launch over the side. By adjusting your feet and hand placement you can manage your speed to be either quite slow or super-fast. The fastest person on record down the mountain was actually a German guy on a bike who clocked in at 172 km per hour. Familia Lundgren didn't break any speed records on our first try but judging by the volcanic pebbles in our eyes and mouths we all hit a respectable pace. We can't wait to go again when friends visit.

We go to the nearby city of León as a family once, sometimes twice, a week. We walk everywhere, because taxi or bicycle cab ride costs add up and besides, León is a really walkable city. When we walk, we are often the cover of the Beatles 1969 classic album, Abbey Road. Cully is Lennon, and Harlan Starr follows closely behind. Olle McCartney is next, with Miriam Harrison usually bringing up the rear. We have shoes on, there aren't a lot of crosswalks in León, and we are usually carrying multicolored grocery bags packed with the week's essentials, but for a moment at least, we feel we are a band, moving and weaving as an out of place rock group to the city's pulse.

Griteria, which literally translates to 'the screaming', or the 'day of yelling' happens every December 7th across Nicaragua. The holiday requires that you learn a phrase, "*quien causa tanta alegria,"* translated as "who is causing so much joy?'. Once you've got that in your tool box, you walk (in our case with a large group of about 14) down the narrow, dusty rounds of El Tololar, dodging cow poop and other groups being pulled on big wagons by horses or oxen. You don't approach every house, only those who have crafted a shrine to Mary somewhere out front, shrines you can usually spot from the road. You walk up, ask where all the joy is coming from, and the home's occupants reply, "*la Concepcion de Maria,*" or 'the Virgin Mary.'

Many of the homes for Mary are absolutely beautiful, and you can inspect them more deeply while bumbling through one of several traditional songs in Spanish. Each house that has a shrine is required by law (okay, by custom) to give you something in return. In this sense it is really both a Catholic holiday and also a day for the community to come together, and for those who have been blessed with more to give back. It's kind of a mixture between Christmas caroling and Halloween, because in addition to singing you bring a sack with you that is filled by the homeowners with candy, really sugary dried papaya, sweet drinks called yuppies, lollipops, bags of popcorn, and even large plastic bowls and cups, gifts that have come in very handy in our kitchen.

Our *Griteria* experience started earlier in the day with Miriam, Carlos and Marilyn giving us a large plate of food for lunch, a traditional meal of chicken (the same chicken Miriam had killed that morning), vegetables, rice, and even a few raisins for sweetness. Round 1 of "*pollo relleno*" was really delicious, as was round 2, the exact same meal being delivered two hours later by Paula and Santo, who live on the other side of Adilsa.

We began our *Griteria* walk with mostly full bellies which became totally full during the two-hour walk by virtue of copious sweets, many of which were consumed en route. Yader, Fernando and Jessica, who passed by on motorcycle in the dark, insisted that we stop by their house on our way home. We did, and after some small talk, four heaping plates of *pollo relleno* along with two large slices of bread were carried out. You know that feeling you get after Thanksgiving dinner when you can barely move and are happy to just lay on the couch and lapse into a mini-food coma? We had that, squared and possibly cubed, a feeling of fullness that was magnified in a not so positive way by Momma Yader's retelling of the ingredients of her version of the meal, which included at least four freshly killed chickens, various parts of other chickens, undisclosed cuts of pig, and *gaseosa* (soda), the real origin of the dishes' sweetness.

We stumbled home from *Griteria*, less wondering who caused all the joy than what caused all our stomachaches. Actually, being part of *Griteria* was really special for our whole family, a slice of local culture. Not needing to eat for the next two days was just a bonus!

Miriam is a nurse, no question about it. We mentioned previously that she came to Leo's aid when the side of Don Leonel's house made a small hole in his head during a soccer game. Since then, Miriam has taken care of the other Miriam's finger when she accidentally stapled it, tended to Carlos's foot after a thorn sliced it during a nighttime motorcycle ride, and massaged Adilsa. She has re-wrapped Miriam's stomach wound multiple times after gallbladder surgery, re-bound Mariela's bandage after wrist surgery, and cleaned Harlan and Olle's numerous cuts and scrapes, including one Harlan got falling out of a coconut tree during a game of hide and seek. Most recently, our friend Maynor came over – clearly the word that Flo Nightingale was in the house had spread – seeking help in cleaning a nasty cut that required several stitches he got playing barefoot soccer with friends.

Everyone seems to know to come to Nurse Mimi, both because of her attentiveness and compassion, and because she brought with her to Nicaragua an arsenal of healing products that rivals the clinic in El Tololar. When not playing nurse, she has acted as the resident pharmacist, dispersing various medications, including most recently allergy pills and pain medication to Don Leonel, who was suffering from post-hernia surgery groin pain, aggravated by excessive, seasonal allergy-induced sneezing. She has also doled out drugs to our whole family; we've collectively been hit with bad seasonal allergies, likely because of the recent change from winter to summer. Allergies fall into that "we can deal for a while but this just really sucks on top of other hardships" category. Given the way life unfolds in Nicaragua, Miriam's skills will continue to come in handy for sure.

The Christmas season 'feel' in Nicaragua is very different for us in a couple of ways. First, the stark difference between what we have and what our neighbors have in terms of material possessions is especially apparent. One neighbor was surprised that the lights we bought to string on our patio cost about $4. None of the other neighbors have lights (or Christmas trees for that matter) because in El Tololar if you have $4 you don't buy lights, you buy rice and beans. You don't pay $5 for an extension cord, you just fix your crappy old one – with a machete (for the 20th time). In El Tololar, a few bucks is substantial, and people know where to put it to the best use.

It's also a bit hard to get into the Christmas season when it's 90 degrees out, although we are not complaining, and the only snow is termite dust from above or from the makeshift snow-making machine Olle crafted one day by rubbing a piece of wood against another, "Look Ma, snow!" The most festive holiday music we hear from our neighbors (other than *Felice Navidad* when shopping in La Union grocery store in León) is Esteban's oft downright gaudy selection of local and international favorites, blared at various hours of the day. We asked Harlan and Olle what were some of the things they miss most about the season: cookies, the smell of home, lighting candles, friends, decorations, food, neighbors, skiing, and of course, family.

We attended the El Tololar High School *promoción* (graduation) recently as special guests and representatives of Tololamos. Thirty-nine secondary school students graduated (high school here lasts basically through 11th grade). Two of the students, including Slilma and Xochilt, one of our other scholarship recipients, will have the chance to go to college thanks to funds provided with the help of our friends.

Prior to the actual ceremony, there was a 'pre-ceremony' at the local Catholic church. We stood in the back and tried to understand the pastor but only could catch a word here and there. Near the end of the ceremony, a commotion at the rear of the sanctuary caught our attention. We turned around to see a 5-foot *ratonera* (mouse killer) snake (our friend Chico gave a positive ID) slurking (slither-lurking) near the wall. Those around us were amused for a moment, and Olle got a little close for comfort ("Look Ma, snake") but a snake in church is just not that big a deal, and the service continued. At the high school (right next door), the graduation itself went off without a hitch, except for when *Familia Lundgren* missed our cue to sit in the special guest section, requiring that we walk – Beatles-style – across the courtyard with hundreds of eyes on the four *gringos*. Graduating from high school in Nicaragua is a very big deal, and it was a special experience to witness this big day for so many students whom we have come to know.

There is something surreal about holding a large plow and standing directly behind two giant bulls while hollering at the oxen, 'stop', 'go', or "other row' in Spanish, sweating profusely and watching sporadic poop fall around you, with a giant volcano smoking in the distance. Cully found himself in this very situation recently after having been invited by Nestor to continue to experience the whole process of yuca cultivation. Thus far the procedure has included cutting yuca stalks to plant, planting (*sembrando*) yuca, throwing fertilizer on the seedlings, pulling weeds, and now cultivating the soil.

Waking up at 4:20 a.m., Nestor, Carlos, and Cully hopped on the family motorcycle (three grown men can easily fit on a cycle, and we have even seen five of six when you include grandmas and small children) and headed to the home of Nestor's father, Raul. Raul's neighbor had apparently borrowed the bulls, but upon arriving at his house he was found inebriated from the previous night's activities and only capable of grunting that he thought the bulls must be on a walkabout. Nestor hopped on a horse like a real cowboy, and was back within 20 minutes with two bulls in tow.

He showed Cully how to tie the yoke to connect the bulls, and in no time they were cultivating the soil (Cully bent over and in pain, Nestor working the oxen like a champ), using a technique of tilling that has not changed for hundreds, perhaps a thousand years. It has been a privilege and a huge learning experience for us, to see the challenges that farmers like Nestor face here every day, and to taste a small bit of it. The life of a Nicaraguan farmer is exceedingly hard and we hope that our involvement with Tololamos in its health, education and environment projects (all of which are either directly or indirectly connected to farming as El Tololar's heart continues to beat to an agrarian drum) will have a positive impact on people like Nestor.

Nestor, and the whole Rivas family, do not have easy lives. They've lived here on the property where we live for about 25 years. When they first moved here, they built Don Leonel's house first and for many years, approximately 15 people lived together there. It was even smaller then, and somehow they crammed grandpas, sons, daughters, grandsons and granddaughters, aunts and uncles all into one room to sleep. Fifteen people sleeping in one small room? That's not easy. But they did it. Over the years, whenever they could scrape up enough money, they would build another house for another family member, always completing the work themselves.

They built latrines. Latrine-building is an interesting multi-week, multi-person process that involves using horses to cart the dirt away and digging down, one shovel full at a time, to a depth of about 8 meters before constructing the frame with aluminum panels. They also planted fruit trees, dug wells, and simply lived together, as one unit, with no electricity or running water until about 10 years ago. More houses were added, ours being the most recent, and it will be gifted to our neighbor Miriam's children when we leave. More family members were born, others died or moved away. Through it all they remain a family unit, and they have each other's backs, always. In the past 3½ months, we have been blessed to know that they have our backs too and vice-versa.

Miriam doing laundry "Nica"style.

Miriam and Adilsa making homemade tortillas.

Olle running in the nearby peanut field.

Carlos knows his corn.

The baseball boys.

Cully and Harlan in front of our little house.

Harlan and Olle with their friends at school.

Our friends and Nicaraguan family.

After a Sunday "juego de futbal."

Nestor and Miriam healing an infected vampire bat bite.

Miriam's parents delivering medical supplies - and Olle's photo bomb!

The Mariano bus breaks down.

Miriam and the boys on their way to school.

Olle after a long afternoon of playing in the volcanic soil.

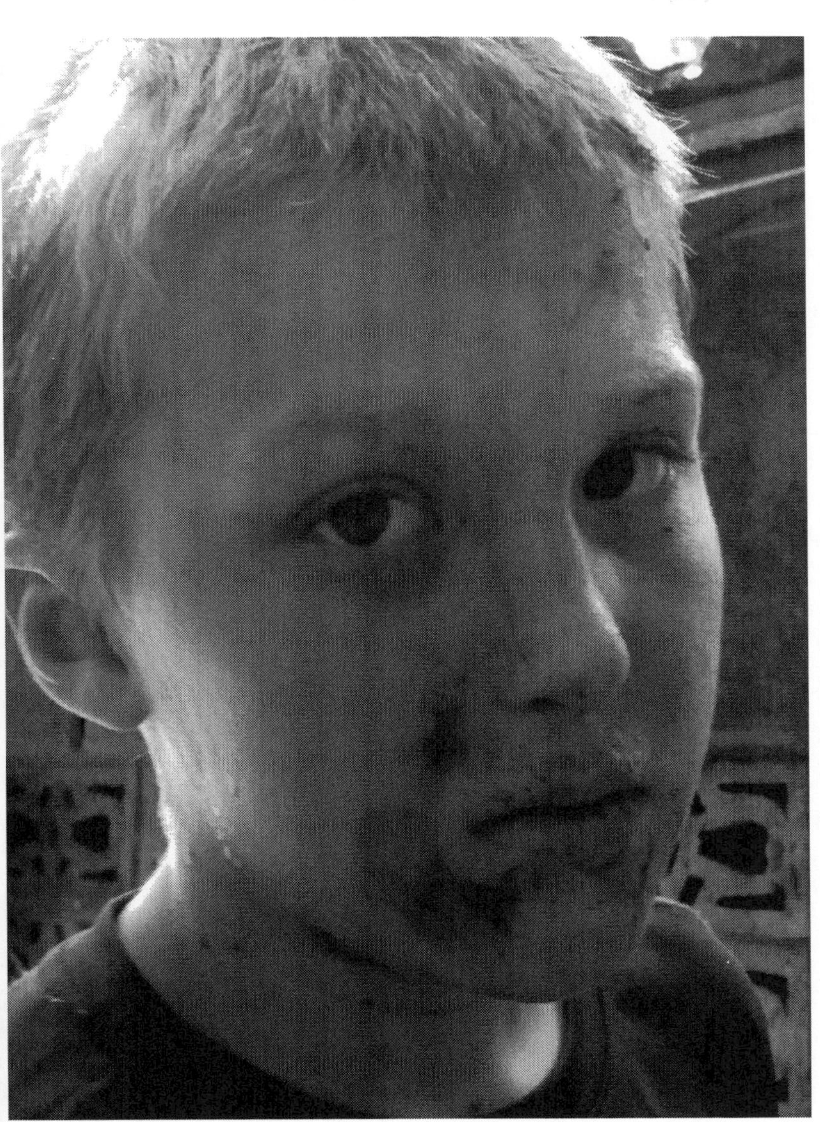

A dirty Harlan.

Primer Carrera de Tololamos.

Cooking with our dear friend Ivania.

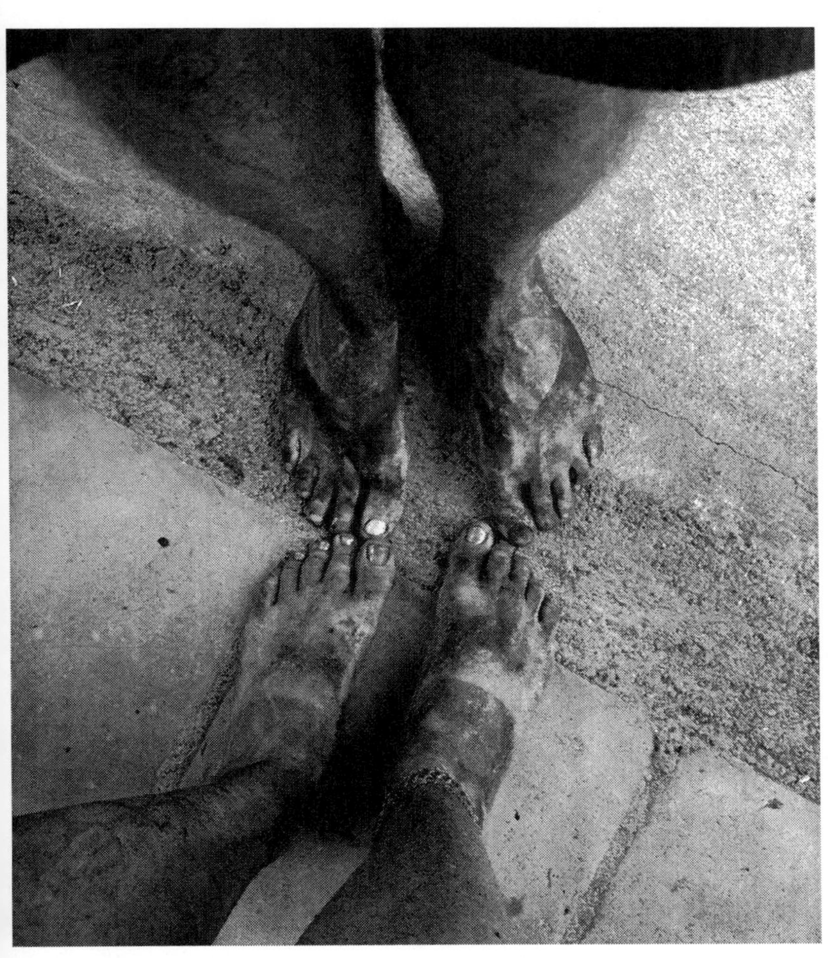

Feet after a soccer game.

Cully, Harlan and Olle with the families of Tololamos scholarship students.

Miriam, Harlan and Olle helping plant seedlings for the tree nursery project of Tololamos.

Chapter 11:
Wild Horses, Market Gazing, Adios Mrs. Chicken

Mid/Late December

When a frog jumps onto your patio during the dry season out of nowhere, you know it's time to terminate the on-again, off-again body of water near your house, dubbed "Lake Lundgren" by Olle. Since we arrived in September, every time we do laundry – usually it's Miriam – a small swamp forms just outside our shower, the low point of our yard. During a big laundry day (say four days' worth of clothes, most of which are downright filthy because of the volcanic soil and dust), Lake Lundgren can get pretty big and when water from four daily showers and washing dishes combines (our house was built so that everything drains to the same place) it can be a legitimate bog. In the rainy season, it often remains for days.

During a recent de-weeding, ant-infested raking session near the lake, we finally had enough. Not only was it getting really smelly, but we were worried that it might provide a breeding ground for mosquitoes, who up till now had made only sporadic visits. We borrowed a shovel and a *cova* (awesome tool that breaks up even the hardest of rocks) and together Miriam and Cully built two matching channels, one leading away from the shower-sink hole, the other from where the laundry water pools. Thanks to a little engineering, Lake Lundgren is no more, in its stead are Moat Olle and Moat Harlan, which we are monitoring closely after each water use to verify that the engineers we hired were worth it.

Our family has received at least 50 or 60 wasp stings since we arrived. It usually seems to be Harlan (often while just sitting innocently in one of our four rocking chairs) or Miriam (usually doing laundry) that get stung the most, although both Olle and Cully have had their share of stings. One wasp stung Cully in his mouth during a soccer game. Another sting, while working at Chico's house, pierced Cully's upper lip, making it exceedingly difficult to adequately relay his experience about raking peanuts for future consumption by Don Leonel's horses to the family one morning.

There are many different kinds of wasps (huge black ones with a really loud buzz, tiny black ones that frequent our kitchen window, more traditional yellow-jacket looking ones) and sometimes it's easiest just to assume they are all dangerous. Again, people from El Tololar are generally not scared in the least. Wilmar must have had 25 of the small black ones and 3 or 4 yellow-jacket looking ones (later found to be *conchitas*) surrounding him when he did laundry one morning. He very nonchalantly explained that the *conchitas* could in fact produce a pretty good sting but that the black ones were no problem unless you really aggravated them, almost demonstrating the type of provocation he was talking about for Cully and Miriam. Co-existence has a special meaning here in Nicaragua; insects and animals we loathe and instinctively reach for the spray bottle to kill at home, are simply allowed to be.

Add veterinarian to the list of Miriam's medical talents. A few days before Christmas, Nestor's horse Blanco (we thought Blanco was Don Leonel's but apparently he was just horse-sitting for Nestor) came walking back home. He had been gone for about a month, having left one day to graze, as he often was allowed to do, and not come back. Nestor and Carlo had taken the moto out several times on unsuccessful reconnaissance missions and they had given up hope that Blanco would ever be found. When he reappeared one afternoon, his ribs were showing even more than usual – most cows, dogs, and horses here are pretty skinny to begin with – and he had a mean looking wound on his back, right where his mane ends.

At first it looked like just a bunch of bloody dirt but as Nestor cleaned it, a much larger gash was revealed, accompanied by a horrific smell of rotting, infected flesh. Several smaller cuts and scrapes were near the large wound and the general consensus was that it was the result of a fight and a bite from another horse. Others thought it may have also been a vampire bat, matching the exact location where Don Leonel's horse had been sucked. Nestor and Miriam took turns cleaning the lesion and pushing out the copious amounts of pus, while Blanco tried to lick it, shivered with pain when they touched it, and bucked or scraped his feet in protest.

Marden arrived unannounced and quickly returned with a cleanser he had used on his pigs that he thought would work as an antiseptic. The triumvirate of Marden, Miriam, and Nestor cleaned, scraped, inspected and disinfected the gash, all the while assuring Blanco that everything would be okay. They worked for almost two hours, past twilight and into the darkness, undeterred by multiple mosquito bites, a flock of chickens in the trees above them, and the frequent fly-bys by a local family of bats, roosting along with the chickens in the nearby trees. Once they cleaned Blanco's wounds, they turned their attention to Don Leonel's horse, whose vampire bat bite wound still hadn't fully healed.

The rainy season has officially ended, and it is summer in El Tololar. That means that we won't get any more measurable rain until at least May, and that the heat will start to gradually increase, reaching a sweaty, dusty, needing multiple showers a day apex by late April, or so we are told. Summer here is also accompanied by strong winds, which started in mid-December, much earlier than normal. The wind can be really powerful and quite dangerous. It knocked over our dinky Christmas tree (along with Fernando's Christmas ornament balls) that we had unsuccessfully duct-taped to the floor on multiple occasions (not so bad), and blew down a large, metal section of our rain gutter, almost onto Miriam's head (not so good). The wind blows pollen and dust around a lot, requiring the Lundgren family to be on a 24-hour regimen of allergy medication, and also necessitating an additional budget line item for tissues (usually paper towels and toilet paper).

The dry, windy weather makes our clothes dry pretty fast, as long as we can locate them after they fly off our clothesline and onto the ant-infested ground, clothespins taking first position on our current week's shopping priority list. It wasn't long ago that we longed for dry weather during a midnight rain-sweeping session on our patio, and now we'd pay a few *cordobas* just to see a little rain. That's life here in a small, impoverished Nicaraguan village. Never easy. You deal with the challenges (be they weather, health, education or job-related), and you rely on family and friends for help.

A Haitian proverb is the title of author Tracy Kidder's excellent book *Mountains Beyond Mountains.* It is significant because it really makes sense for all of us, no matter where we live. The proverb basically says that we shouldn't expect things to get easy. Life is not about arriving at a destination but about a process of growth, and of meeting challenges head-on. We hike one mountain (or experience a difficulty in life) and we should be ready for the next challenge (or mountain), because as sure as the sun rises, it will be waiting for us, rising in the distance. At first glance the proverb can seem depressing or uninspired, "So you mean life is just a series of trials and tribulations, one after the other?" one might say. "Where is the fun in that?" But when you really think about it, the proverb can invigorate us and provide a context for a life of purpose. We wake each day with a mountain in front of us. It is not an obstacle, but an opportunity—an opportunity to be the best hiker we can be that day, to hike mountains not alone but in community with others. For us, life in Nicaragua is a mountain and an opportunity. And there will be another mountain waiting for us when we return and re-enter life in the states, in some ways the biggest challenge of our trip. What is your next mountain?

Recently, we walked by a boy in the crowded market near the cathedral in León. He was laying on his back in front of his mother's food stall, looking up at the sky with a serene face as people bumped, jostled, and shoved their way past, many likely oblivious to his presence. What was the boy thinking? What was he dreaming of? Maybe it was his love (like ours) of city markets, lively places, the hearts of many cities, where people from all walks of life come to buy and sell, jumbled together in a miasma of *rainbowic* (it should be a word) colors and smells. The cathedral market place (León's cathedral is the oldest in Central America) is a place where you can (and will) find most anything, especially food. Piping hot, steamy soups with hunks of meat-covered bone of unknown origin (Cully thumbs up, Miriam thumbs down), freshly made corn tortillas, delicious fruit juices squeezed before your eyes, fried chicken and pork, accompanied by various sauces, and sweets, lots of local breads and desserts that can make you fat just by looking at them.

Maybe the boy on his back was dreaming about his next meal, what he would eat for lunch on that bright sunshiny day (that is if his mom could make enough that morning selling tortillas). Or maybe he was daydreaming about someday going to college, if his mom could sell many more tortillas. Maybe we all have a little bit of daydreaming in us, a need for a space to look up, to allow the busyness of life to pass us by for a moment, while we imagine possibilities…

Caramelo the pig, a 200-pound sow, gave birth to five piglets, all breach, between about 8 p.m. and midnight on December 23rd. We knew Caramelo was pregnant, but assumed she still had a few weeks to go. But when Carlos came over asking for our ant killer spray to rid the birthing area she was preparing of biting ants, we knew her time had come. After dinner we, along with various members of the Rivas family, set up shop outside Caramelo's quarters, some sitting in chairs, others standing, chatting or cheering each time the massive pig moved or grunted. It was like watching a baseball game – similar starting time – or a movie. Miriam even considered making popcorn. The cheers got louder at about 8:25 p.m., when our neighbor Miriam came over to tell us that piggy number 1 had been born (Harlan and Olle had just bedded down themselves). We went right over as number 2 was getting ready.

It was a comical scene. The two Miriams on either side of Caramelo, petting, whispering encouragement, and gently helping her push. Carlos was playing catcher at her rear end, calling out directions ("one more push, a little harder, inside curveball"). Cully and the boys to the pig's side were videoing and likewise providing verbal encouragement. After several brief appearances of legs, a few final pushes by Caramelo and the Miriams, and a nice pull by Carlos, a slimy, pink oinker popped out. Her eyes were closed, and she spent the next 30 minutes attempting to suckle, usually unsuccessfully, in part because every several minutes one of Adilsa's dogs would attempt to get a closer look. Figaro, Adilsa's kitten who is really cute but gets into everything, kept attacking the newly born pig's still attached umbilical cord, thinking it was some sort of special treat.

The whole experience was new for us, and we couldn't help but think it was like a version of the Christmas story, being surrounded as we were, perhaps like Baby Jesus, by pigs, cows, dogs, chickens, and cats. Actually, it really was like the Christmas story. Mary, like Caramelo, giving birth amidst the dirt and dust of a barn, the bright, rural stars shining overhead. In that sense our friends here in many ways have a much better understanding then we do of the meaning of Christmas, experiencing the dirty, raw, organic nature and reality of life in a visceral way, every day.

The day after Caramelo gave birth, we witnessed death. A big Christmas dinner was being planned, and six chickens were to be slaughtered for the feast the day before. We missed the demise of the first two, only coming upon two limp, still feathery birds when Adilsa called us over from across the fence line to help her pluck. We spent a good 30 minutes chatting and plucking breasts, heads, wings and butts, stopping only to wash the sticky feathers from our fingers. We did see the third death.

We had been sitting and chatting with the family, having just exchanged Christmas gifts. Carlos was sitting in a chair, listening intently while stroking a chicken sitting on his lap. At some point he got up and called us to come around to the back yard, where we witnessed a few neck swipes by his machete. Once the blood had drained, Adilsa brought the chicken into the kitchen to show us how you get it ready to pluck, plopping it in a boiling pot of water just long enough to make feather removal easier. We always knew those plump breasts you buy at the supermarket came from somewhere, and this experience gave us a better appreciation for the work and sacrifice that goes into it.

No one really takes much time to name their animals here, largely because they aren't expected to stay around that long. Even getting Caramelo the pig's name out of Carlos was tough, him seeming to make up the name on the spot to please us. But we have named Adilsa's two dogs on our own, initially erroneously and now just because it's kind of funny. They are *Sale* (we pronounce it Sally) and *Fuera*. '*Sale*' basically means leave, and '*Fuera*' means outside. The two dogs just don't understand boundaries, and want to always be part of the action. Hence whenever a few people are gathered chatting, you often here the names (actually commands) 'SALE', 'FUERA'. For some reason the little dog gets told to leave more, while the larger one gets told to go outside, and so to us, they are Sally and Fuera. They are cute dogs, but have a habit of itching themselves, eating our cat food, digging in our garbage and hunting our rabbit, and so we are happy to continue to, affectionately, tell them to leave and go outside.

Olle loves little things, especially animals—one reason we now have a large rabbit in our kitchen that eats and poops too much and most likely a pregnant kitten with morning sickness that lolls about all day on our bed. They were both really cute when we got them though. That desire for another small animal, this time a baby chicken, sent Cully and Wilmar on a nighttime motorcycle ride through the dusty streets of Tololar in search of a chick, a *pollito*. They first asked at the house nearby that breeds chickens. They only had one left, and it was sick. It was suggested that it would be good to inquire at another house, but they only had a really little chicken that still required its mother for warmth.

It must have been strange, two people knocking on your door out of the blue in the dark, with the strange query. "Hi, I'm the new gringo who lives down the street. You may have seen my family and me over the past few months on the bus, or running in the peanut field. Yeah, well, my son wants a baby chicken for Christmas, and we thought you might have one. Can you help me?" The nighttime chicken run was ultimately unsuccessful, and so our house remains occupied by only two juvenile animals. For the time being, Olle has to be content playing with – and then sometimes eating – our neighbors' chickens.

Grandma and Grandpa's arrival on December 26th was as anticipated an event as any of us can remember. We'd been in Nicaragua for just over four months and we (especially the boys) were absolutely giddy about getting to be with Grandma and Grandpa, the boys understanding that undoubtedly Grams and Gramps would fulfill their relational duty to spoil their grandkids, which they did with gusto. They rented a 4x4 truck (very smart move) and together we drove through and around Managua, León, El Tololar, and the nearby beach communities of Poneloya and Las Peñitas. We only got really lost on New Year's Eve in Managua, receiving no less than 5 sets of different directions before Grandpa had the brilliant idea of hailing a taxi to escort us to our destination.

We laughed, cried, swam, ate, drank, walked, drove, and sung our way to an amazing week that proved to be a much needed refresher and morale booster for all of us. And thanks to multiple hot showers, *Familia* Lundgren came away cleaner than we'd been since August! We are so thankful for the generosity of spirit that Grandma and Grandpa shared with us and with El Tololar. They came to our house on two occasions to get a sense of our life here, and the whole Rivas family loved them, remarking on multiple occasions on how young they seemed. They were also duly impressed with Grandpa's soccer playing skills!

Perhaps the most rewarding part of Grandma and Grandpa's visit was a stop at the health center in El Tololar on their last day. The center's doctor had previously given us a wish list of medical supplies that they most needed. Grandpa had found a way to requisition virtually all of it. He and Grandma 'smuggled' the goods into the country – along with lots of soccer balls and baseball gloves, the gloves for some reason receiving the greatest scrutiny by customs officials, as if their true intention was to initiate a covert baseball league that might one day play a role in overthrowing the government – and brought a huge duffel bag to carry them all. They included everything from glucose strips, to surgical gloves, to stethoscopes, bandages, suture kits, and a baby scale. The doctor, who had a chance to see these goods only after Grandma and Grandpa had left, was over the moon. Small things, big impact. *Gracias, Gracias, Gracias!!*

What's the big deal about a chair? Normally, not much. But when twelve plastic chairs, two rocking chairs, two fans and a table show up at a health center where people previously were forced to sit on the floor or a concrete slab while they waited for medical attention, butts (especially) and their owners get really happy. A good friend of ours provided funds for the above supplies, which we were privileged to help deliver to the health center along with our Tololamos friends, Beto and Adilsa. Two women with babies were escorted to the rocking chairs, the plastic chairs were quickly occupied, and the doctor (she is awesome) came out to thank Tololamos. Another patient made her own remarks about how big of a deal a chair really is to a sick person. Small things, big impact.

Asking for directions in another language and country is always an experience, especially so when flat tires get involved. Grandma and Grandpa Muntz had just treated us to an amazing mangrove forest boat ride cruise that included about thirty sightings of various local birds, a possible but unconfirmed crocodile sighting, a lone raccoon, several large termite nests, a golden orb spider, and four recently born baby turtles at a hatchery that were awaiting their release into the ocean that afternoon. Upon parking for lunch, Miriam noticed that the rear, right tire of our rental truck was mostly flat. The parking lady told Cully that there was a tire fix-it place in the next town and while the others waited, he set off.

An elderly, toothless man relayed that down the road, in the other direction, there were in fact two tire repair shops, both recognizable by old tires set on the side of the road. The first tire sign was a bike tire, and the staff (a father and son working out of their house) instructed Cully to continue on to the next, larger sign, at which point he should turn to the left and ask for Javier. Some 200 yards further was the sizeable car-tire size sign, but upon turning onto a small dirt road, none of the four children playing soccer knew anyone named Javier who fixed tires. Cully followed a separate lead down another road, only to encounter a dead-end and a police station across a fence line. None of the cops were aware of any nearby tire stores, but felt pretty confident that a guy named Lollo (Javier was now out of the picture) fixed tires out of his house, located a few streets down. A failed attempt or two later finally brought Cully to a side street and face to face with a smiling Lollo, who filled the tire, diagnosed that it was only a small leak, and promptly charged 100 *cordobas* for the air, and no doubt the experience!

New Year's Day brought us both the departure of Miriam's parents as well as our first official sting by a scorpion. Cully was doing some post-holiday clean-up, and took the opportunity to open the bedroom window to air out the dust and weeks' worth of accumulated bug detritus. He simultaneously saw something move out of the corner of his eye and felt a sting on his right hand. A mid-sized scorpion came into view, falling into a pile of assorted shoes, sandals, boots, and a guitar. Miriam and Cully quickly found the scorpion (*alacron* in Spanish) in the shoe pile and killed it – actually quite easy to do – in short order. Local stories about the power of scorpion stings (about three times as bad as a wasp sting, can make your tongue go numb, severe joint pain, dizziness, etc) came flooding into Cully's head but after a few minutes, his hand had only swollen a skosh and the pain was much less than expected. Somehow, the scorpion had partially missed – more likely from it being startled from its slumber then any lightning-fast reflexes on Cully's part – and we came away with a good story rather than a dusty, afternoon motorcycle ride to the hospital in León.

How dare you chop down those trees? That was our first thought when we heard the buzz of a chainsaw and witnessed three eucalyptus trees falling to the earth, two fence lines over from our house. For goodness' sakes birds live in those trees, but more importantly they provide an excellent background for our morning exercise/quiet times, and the wind that gently caresses their leaves in the morning makes us feel happy, and damn, we just need that little slice of happiness sometimes. But in reality, it's not a big deal to lose those trees, and we aren't so disappointed that our halcyon days of selfish-tree bliss are over. Why? Because those trees, like everything here, serve a purpose. They will be the frame of a new tower, reaching to the sky, replacing the old tower (which after six years succumbed to weather and an army of termites) that holds the water tank that irrigates – and therefore provides life – to Don Leonel's corn field. We lost a couple trees; the family will receive a continued, sustained supply of water to their fields. Ask any farmer, that's a big deal!

P.S. the guy who cut down the trees is a wizard. He used a chainsaw (*motosierra* in Spanish) to not only cut down the tree, but to cut the planks for the tower… perfectly. This guy was like Rembrandt with a saw, carving and creating perfectly, symmetrical planks with a freaking chainsaw. But that is par for the course here. Out of necessity, creativity and artistry are born.

Chapter 12:

Redemption Songs, Baptism by Piñata, Gone with the Wind

Early/Mid-January

During the wet season, the Nicaraguan sky dumped buckets of water on us almost daily. And frequent lightning storms meant that a good deal of time, we were without both electricity and running water. January has brought more stability on the electrical front (we generally have power) but perhaps the heavy winds, a broken water pipe, or some other variable – it can be annoying not knowing which variable – has resulted in us operating without water for the majority of the time since Christmas. When the water does begin to sputter on – usually between 5-7 a.m. – we move into 'water capture' mode, filling our three, 5-gallon containers as quickly as possible. That way we can at least wash dishes, have access to drinking water, and in a pinch, take a much-needed bucket shower after a sweaty, dusty game of soccer.

Living without reliable, constant, effortless access to water is hard. Without water, you actually can't make – gulp – coffee in the morning: egads! Without water, it's really hard to 'dry-wash' your clothes. It's harder to swallow an allergy pill with only your saliva. Without water, you can't wash the vegetables that are part of your dinner plans. But we're learning a lesson; take extra care of the resources you have, because they may not always be there. It's actually a good model to follow for all things, not just natural resources like water. Take good care of your family, your friends, your health, your 'things'. Value and treasure them, always.

A couple Sunday nights back we held one of our monthly movie nights at the house. We told neighbors and friends beforehand and prepped per usual by buying a boatload of soda and making copious amounts of popcorn. Sunday's movie night was a bit more hectic than others. Olle was sick, like really sick, vomiting and not keeping anything down since the night before. Miriam had stayed at our house with Olle prior to the 6 p.m. scheduled showing while a sundry group of ten others threw water on the dusty soccer pitch prior to a pre-movie game to minimize the anticipated levels of dust that would rise from the ground with every kick. The group included Larry, our neighbor, who has already become a soccer legend because of his uncanny ability to fake opponents out of their pants. Not ten minutes into the game, Nestor, playing barefoot as usual, stepped on a sharp rock, opening up a gaping wound near his toe and ending his playing time for the day. Fortunately, in no time his wound was cleaned and bandaged by a sprinting, hydrogen-peroxide, triple antibiotic toting Miriam.

We all returned home and began shuffling chairs, pouring soda, popping final batches of corn, and waiting for our first showing of Star Wars in Spanish. Technical difficulties meant the movie started late, giving us time to greet guests while intermittently checking on Olle. He was sequestered in Miriam and Cully's room and armed with his own Blu-ray player and a barf bucket. About 7:00 p.m., Yader and his sister Jessica showed up on a motorcycle, transporting freshly made salad, *repochetas*, and refried beans lovingly made for us by their mother, Mayra. They were carrying a box containing two, loudly chirping baby chicks, Yader helping to fulfill Olle's

Christmas wish only two weeks tardy. The chicks, one black and one striped white, have since been named '*Pagi*' and '*Malam*'', the words for morning and night in Indonesian (we know, strange…)

There was a lot going on during movie night, what with storm troopers yelling '*adelante*' and Chewbacca being the only one who sounded the same in English and Spanish, and it was such a great example of Olle's generosity of spirit that even in his diminished state he peeped his head out of the room to profusely thank Yader for the two *pollitos.*

After multiple sleep-deprived nights, we finally broke down and ordered a custom-made, hardwood bed, made lovingly by Yader's dad, also named Yader. Our old bed (which was never ours to begin with but our neighbor Belkies') now sits in our kitchen until we can find a new home for it, precariously perched on the brick wall and once falling on our rabbit while sweeping, nearly flattening poor Rainer. The new bed has an absolutely gorgeous, hand-carved frame, and for really a song (about $100) we procured it with only 1 ½ weeks lead time, delivered to our house one afternoon while Miriam's parents were still here, by pony express. It truly is beautiful, but unfortunately it hasn't yet proven to be nearly as comfortable as it looks; next stop – mattress store!

Over the past four plus months, our friend Fernando has already shown us his many talents, most of them artistic in nature. First hand-carved and delicately inscribed bowls made of a local fruit called *jícaro* showed up in two separate installments, followed in short order by a delivery of homemade red, green, gold and silver Christmas ornaments. Two weeks back he showed up with three original paintings, all lovingly carved on the same pale-red roof tiles that beautify many of the our neighbors' roofs, at least those that aren't made of the omnipresent corrugated metal that burns under the noon sun and produces a furious, almost enraged clamor during a rainstorm.

Two dolphins soar toward the water's surface in the painting that hangs near our kitchen. Near Miriam's garden hangs an African elephant, standing majestically in the fading light of the savannah. And in our kitchen, next to our window that overlooks our front yard, sits a lighthouse on a peninsula, surrounded by what looks like the choppy, salty, and yet somehow comforting, wild ocean of the Atlantic. Perhaps unknowingly, or more likely with a profound understanding, Fernando has in his own quiet way given us a deeper sense of place, reminding us of the home we left behind, and the home we have here.

A mystery has been solved. For the past couple months, our rabbit Rainer, a girl we had been told, has been getting increasingly frisky with our cat Dulce, also a girl. Perhaps keeping such as prolific reproducer alone in the kitchen, at times with only an equally frisky cat, is not the best play, but Rainer generally loves the kitchen. She sleeps and spends most of her day there, munching on weeds, cabbages, and carrots, only wanting to get out every morning for a quick look around and a pee. But we have happened upon Rainer and Dulce, underneath our stove or in a corner, taking turns swatting at, sitting atop and jumping on each other, with Rainer often having the upper hand.

Our friend Erickson, the same guy who gifted us Rainer during a downpour two months back, and also generally understood to be the local rabbit whisperer, solved a part of the mystery. Rainer is in fact a boy. Erickson recently declared this while showing Miriam the goods, his initial diagnosis in error only because of the rabbit's young, immature age at the time. We now have at least part of the answer to our increasingly perplexing query, 'Why is our rabbit humping our cat?" But still, as Harlan astutely recently pointed out, 'Why is our *rabbit* humping our *cat*?'

Good Day, Bad Day. We all have good days and bad days, no matter where we live. Here are two examples from our life here in Nicaragua:

GOOD DAY: We wake up early after a restful night, the distant sound of roosters mingling gently in the air with the soft bellow of cows and the occasional far off bark of a dog. Miriam and Cully take forty-five blessed minutes to exercise on our patio under our thatched roof, the soft wind caressing our skin as we stretch to meet the day, armed with plentiful and delicious Nicaraguan coffee. At times we are joined by our cat Dulce (often jumping on Cully's lap), Rainer the bunny (sniffing our toes and keeping a close watch out for dogs) and now our two baby chicks, who snuggle near us for warmth. The sun rises over the mostly fallow corn field, and Olle and Harlan wake up in good spirits. We have a lovely family breakfast of scrambled eggs, bread, and fresh grapefruit we picked off the branch just yesterday, blended with great conversation, a gift of connection for our family that this year has brought.

The school day goes really well, and the boys find a way to concentrate and learn, in spite of the challenges. After school we have a meeting with our neighbor and excellent friend Adilsa and a group of students to whom we are helping provide scholarships. Their smiles of gratitude warm our hearts. We then pick corn with the family in the nearby field, filling sack after sack. We feel good, because we know that corn is used to make just about everything and that this corn will surely not go to waste. We have a soccer game with the whole family in Don Leonel's yard. We laugh, play hard, and get really dirty. Harlan and Olle find more time to play with Rachel and Leo, and then after showering (we have water!!) we eat a delicious meal of rice and beans, or maybe a special and anticipated offering of pasta – with chicken.

Several neighbors stop by during the evening, bringing more food but mostly just sharing of themselves. We speak in Spanish, and on this day the flow of conversation makes us feel like we really know what we are talking about. We fall asleep after relaxing to a part of a really good movie, our room clear of bugs, our bellies full, and our hearts content. We are doing it! Living together as a family in a Nicaraguan village, learning, sharing, and feeling grateful for the experience.

BAD DAY: The wind has howled all night, sounding and feeling like an out of control locomotive, threatening to fling our roof into the nearby cornfield, uprooting leftover mud in our gutter from the wet season and depositing it on our floor, thus making any midnight, blind walks from our bed to our pee bucket that much more perilous. Needless to say we don't sleep much this night.

Upon waking, we are greeted by a mid-sized tarantula on the floor outside our room. We rush to kill it, and then fumble to unlock the kitchen door, dodging bunny poops in the dark and finally finding the tissues; we both have really bad allergies. The constant sneezing and coughing make it hard to focus, or taste the coffee, and Harlan and Olle also wake up dreary-eyed, coughing and sneezing. Our physical disorders are accompanied for some reason this morning by a longing for home, for friends and family, and for a cozy place where the weather cannot find us.

School sucks this day, with many outbursts, frustrations, and seemingly little learning. School sucks partly because the wind continues to blow all morning, powerful gusts hurling palm leaves and dust (*polvo* in Spanish, also known locally as 'yellow snow') all over our porch and into our rooms. After school, we try to eat beans and rice but the beans Miriam cooked two days before have since gone bad because of a day without electricity. The dirty clothes are piling up but we have no water so the mound continues to grow. Harlan and Olle are bored out of their minds in the afternoon, and they pass the time by making a trip to the local *venta*, where they purchase a local sweet drink known as a *yuppi* (dreadfully sweet with a ton of sugar). Olle comes back almost in tears as he stepped on a big biting ant hill unknowingly while making one of several barbed-wire fence crossings.

The wind continues to blow, at times forcing huge waves of smoke from a nearby garbage fire through our entire house. The chicks are cute but insist on walking on our patio, leaving fresh poops wherever they go. By evening we have had enough but the dust prevents us from running as a stress-reliever in the nearby field without having huge coughing fits. We still have no water by dinner and so can't shower, and damn it would feel good to scrub those four layers of dust off. Harlan starts coming down with a stomach bug after dinner, on top of his cold, and the boys go to bed tired and not at all happy to be here. We fall asleep a few hours later, covered in dust, wondering why we are here and praying to God that tomorrow will be a brighter day. As we doze off, the power suddenly comes on, and the lights that we unintentionally left on while we had electricity wake the boys up, ensuring that we are all in for a long, sleepless night. Somewhere in the distance, a rooster crows…

Olle has given us all a gift. Every animal that we either currently have or have come into contact with has come to us based on Olle's desire and dogged determination. First it was Dulce the cat, who was originally Don Leonel's kitten. Don Leonel must have seen the way Olle cared for, held, and caressed the kitten (a type of love and affection for animals that is rarely seen here) and he gifted her to Olle, despite that meaning that he wouldn't have a future mouse hunter under his roof. Next came Rainer the rabbit, and our friend Erickson must have seen the way Olle held and stroked the soft bunny, understanding that he would provide it with a good home and love. Ow-ey the Owl was with us for only a short time (six days), but it was Olle who wanted to care for and nurture the sick, injured bird back to health, despite the odds. Finally came Pagi and Malam the baby chicks, our friend Yader clearly understanding that the smile they brought to Olle, who chased them incessantly as he tried to catch them at Yader's' house one night, was one that could not be ignored but rather needed to be rewarded.

Initiating a mini-farm at our house was not our original intention, and at times having animals in this environment can be irritating. Every day we have lots of rabbit pee and chicken poop to scoop off our patio or from our kitchen floor, mouse entrails and half lizards greet us in the morning, and loud meowing and soon possibly cock-a-doodle-dooing noises are all part of the package. But in the end, they have brought us a little piece of joy. It feels good to cuddle with a rabbit on a rainy night, or listen to the *purr* of a cat on your lap, or to just watch as a baby chick chirps or as she pecks at things to learn about the world around her. Thanks for the animals, Olle!

UPDATE: Catching baby chicks is not easy. Miriam and Cully have a new ritual, chasing Pagi and Malam around our patio every night in order to put them to sleep in our kitchen-based chicken hutch. They are incredibly fast, and only by a concerted team effort involving lots of yelling directions and multiple errant, unsuccessful dives (we feel kind of like border collies herding sheep) do we finally get them to bed.

The *Fiesta Patronal*, or Party of the Saints, happens in El Tololar every year on the second weekend of January. It is a big deal, and from what we can tell one of the biggest community events of the year. Last week we had the opportunity to attend several events associated with the day, arriving Saturday evening at the Catholic Church with a small group of family and friends just in time to see the Virgin Mary knock her head on the doorway as the 10 young men and women carrying her attempted to squeeze she and her entire float through the church entrance. We entered to a church rocking to various music styles that somehow fit despite their lack of congruence. Rapidly shifting from zydeco to polka to R&B sounding music, we swayed and lifted our hands with the rest of the congregation. We largely failed at hearing many actual words except for the extortion, in Spanish, to "stomp on the head of the devil", which we did with relish. It was part square-dancing, part old-school evangelical (although a Catholic ceremony) tent revival, and part sermon, all led by a singing, stomping, sweating and enthusiastic Father (S*acerdote* in Spanish).

Upon leaving the sanctuary, we saw before us a traveling carnival. There were four rides, none of which would likely have passed any safety standards in the US. This was especially true for the high speed 'swing' that Harlan and Olle tried once, whipping you around and around at higher and higher angles, threatening to either launch you towards the church or the health clinic, or into the crowd of on-looking spectators. Perhaps the most aptly named amusement was '*El Titanic*', a scary looking watercraft ride that truly looked like it might sink at any moment. Adilsa's dog had followed us from her house, as she does every time we go anywhere. *Sale* succeeding in being the only animal to actually gain admission into the service. There were tons of dogs outside later at the carnival, however, and we remarked that the only reason they didn't actually attend the service was because they were likely Baptist, not Catholic dogs.

Redemption and forgiveness in action: we saw some last week, and hope to see more soon. The forgiveness happened really as a result of Adilsa and Wilmar. They were in the process of identifying the best candidates for the scholarships our family and friends are helping us to provide to two university students and five high school students this year. They were narrowing down the list, and we came to the name of a young man who had spent many afternoons at our house playing with Olle and Harlan when we first arrived. We'll call him Jorge.

Jorge and his sister didn't speak much English, but they had been so genuinely interested in us, spending whole afternoons at our house, chatting, playing with the boys, and generally just providing pleasant company. One afternoon, after a game of soccer, we came back to our house to find Cully's phone missing. After a day or two of inquiries, we came to find out that in fact Jorge had taken it, telling his friends that it was a gift to him from the '*gringo*'.

We were mad at first, but when we saw his name on the scholarship students list that Adilsa and Wilmar presented, we changed our tune. The incident also provided us the opportunity as a family to discuss on a deeper level about what forgiveness really means, and why is it so hard to actuate. When someone has wronged you, our first response is often revenge, or anger, or hatred. But the act of forgiving someone, often only possible through faith, is so simple yet so hard. It cannot only literally lift a weight off our shoulders, but we can play a part in redeeming another, and likewise lighten their load, instantaneously. Jorge and his family don't have much at all in the way of material things. In fact, they are likely one of the poorer families in El Tololar. Yet Jorge is a really bright student at school, and he, like everyone, deserves a second chance; he deserves redemption and forgiveness. Thank you to our friends and family for helping, from afar, to redeem and forgive.

Part of learning about another culture is to experience as many cultural events as possible. Since we arrived in el Tololar we have attended multiple church services, gone with our family to the cemetery on the Day of the Dead, sang and walked our way through El Tololar during the *Griteria* Festival on December 7th, attended a *Quinceañera* (15th birthday party for local girls, a really big deal), spent a rocking Christmas with local family and friends, and now also attended a post-baptism (*bautismo*) party.

The *Bautismo* party took place at the home of Mariano, one of the two local bus drivers we have become friendly with here in El Tololar. We received an invite the week before, delivered via motorcycle by his grandson. Our intention was to arrive in '*nica time*' – in other words late – and we sauntered up the dirt driveway to the house 25 minutes later than the 3:30 p.m. scheduled start. Clearly we weren't *Nica* enough as we were still some of the first to arrive.

We spent the next hour or more just sitting and watching families slowly saunter in, with the festivities finally getting going about 5:00 p.m.. The main event came first, which was of course the *piñata* smashing. They had two *piñatas*, the first lasting only up until the fourth child took a solid, candy-inducing whack. The second one lasted much longer, starting out as a cute white dog with a green hat. Multiple kids took their turn (we think Harlan and Olle were just too old as the average whacker was about 5 or 6) and by the time they had gone around the circle of chairs, the poor doggy was hanging there, legless, multiple holes in his sides and head. He apparently still had a cavity of candy in him, as the kids kept whacking despite his sorry state. After the *piñatas* came food (plates of rice, bread and chicken that took 45 minutes to deliver to the 200 or so guests), then soda, then ice cream, then goodie bags for the kids.

We went from the post-baptism party to our friend Yader's 20th birthday hoedown, which basically just consisted of a large table set in his front patio, reserved for our family. Multiple plates of foods and soda were delivered to us, as somehow we had become the honored guests. That's rural Nicaraguan hospitality, being given a place of honor at someone else's birthday party. As we have done now on multiple occasions, we ambled home, our bellies full to the brim but thankful for the incredible kindness that is constantly heaped upon us.

Chapter 13:
Crossing the Line, Torching the Wart, Hunting the Beast

Late January

Verruga Vulgar – scary sounding words regardless of the language, especially when they come out of a doctor's mouth in a foreign country at the end of a rather long diagnosis concerning a foot ailment. But such were the final words of Dr. Carlos Pacheco Paiz, delivered just before he began unscrewing a large canister of volatile liquid that smoked profusely as it collided with the hot Nicaraguan air. Harlan and Cully had gone to the second floor of a nondescript physician's office in León seeking a consult for the wart on Harlan's left foot that had steadily grown in the past couple months. Medical treatment was a must because while largely painless if untouched, the wart screamed in pain whenever it was hit by anything. Usually this was a ball or foot colliding with Harlan's, either on the soccer pitch or while trying to squeeze between riders, money collectors, or the plethora of ice cream, vegetable, fried plantain, or soda hawkers on the El Tololar- León bus.

After opening the large container of liquid nitrogen, Dr. Pacheco Paiz began transferring it to a smaller, more manageable thermos, pouring the steaming liquid into the small opening with semi-steady hands, spilling only a little on the tile floor below. Harlan's eyes grew wider with each fluid transfer, no doubt in his mind questioning how the good doctor meant to administer the super sub-zero liquid to his foot. Fortunately the end of the thermos possessed a small-spray hose that would ensure that only Harlan's wart, and not his entire foot, would be frozen. After two separate spray sessions with a few minutes in between, the procedure was complete. The doctor provided assurances that all would be fine, and to expect the wart to blacken and fall off in short order. Trusting someone you don't know with an integral part of your body, regardless of their qualifications, requires a certain sense of courage and Harlan gets huge props for putting his feet in Dr. Paiz's hands.

Before we arrived in Nicaragua, hunting was the last activity in our imagination we thought we'd be taking part. But the following account is proof positive the improbable becomes possible when you live outside your comfort zone:

They were tracking it through the jungle-like forest that had long since swallowed up the road that formerly served as a major thoroughfare in El Tololar. A posse of eight they were, four of whom possessed the instincts of a bloodhound, having hunted the beasts with slingshots and rocks on many occasions before. Here and there were telltale signs that a giant one had passed by recently, visible to the experienced eye in the long, smooth trails left on the dusty soil by its huge tail. Forty-five minutes into the hunt, the beast was still nowhere to be seen, but they were sure it could see them, watching intently as it lay hidden in the trees above.

They crossed the abandoned road, dodging foxholes, stumps and roots, and wasp nests, arriving at a stand of giant eucalyptus trees swaying to the rhythm of the late morning breeze. Suddenly, the champion tracker raised his weapon toward the sky, placed a rough-hewn rock in its pouch, and launched it towards the branches above. A giant green *Gorobo*

fell from the tree, running toward them at an astonishing speed, only to be stopped in its tracks by the mottled brown and black dog that had accompanied them on the hunt. Later that afternoon, they along with the rest of the family gorged themselves on successive bowls of soup, flavored with an array of colorfully-named local vegetables, such as the *quequisque*, and the tasty meat of the behemoth dragon they had slayed that morning.
DISCLAIMER: This story has been slightly embellished for your reading pleasure but most or all of it, in some form or another, actually took place.

From the Desk of Olle:

Living in Nicaragua, I have noticed many differences between Nicaragua and Milton, Massachusetts.

1. Sometimes, we play soccer and after the games, I am hot and dirty, but I can't take a shower because we don't have water. I either have to take a bucket shower or go to the house that usually has well-water. In Nicaragua, our water is always cold and sometimes (hard to believe), I just want a hot shower, but I have to wait till we get back home to Milton.

2. Our neighbors Carlos and Miriam, spend all day on their hammock. Then one day they needed rope for the horse. They used the rope from their hammock for the horse, leaving them without a hammock. They couldn't replace the rope because they needed money for food. People here only buy things they need. In the United States most people can afford to buy what they need and what they want.

3. Here in Nicaragua, we take buses to get anywhere. The buses are old school buses from the USA. I always feel weird on the bus because I am not a local and our family are the only gringos on the bus. In Milton, the buses are nice but I don't need to go on buses there because we have a car, which is easier and quicker. I have learned Nicaragua is different than the USA.

The best $66 we ever spent! At least that's what we told ourselves. We had actually done our homework and found that we could in fact change our visa (we need to do so every 90 days) at the Honduran Border instead of the Costa Rican one. Or so we thought. Our arrival at the border went swimmingly. We took a taxi from the beautiful town of Somoto with a young man named Yader. We exchanged numbers, just in case it took longer than expected, but the short line and bounty of border agents made it look like a quick crisscross was a sure thing; thirty, forty minutes tops to go across into Honduras and back.

The first gentleman *(caballero in Spanish)* who checked our passports was very pleasant, and when we provided a quick summary of our border crossing plans, he seemed supportive of the idea. Things went downhill from there.

Our conversation with the Nicaraguan border agents was tough on multiple levels – language, ambient noise, misinformation, and a little misdirection. Add all of these up and you have unsavory, muddled soup of confusion. We paid our exit fee of $4 each to leave the country, and then walked confidently up the hill towards Honduras. There, two kind agents confirmed what the previous agents had been trying to tell us – you guys can't cross the border here and then re-enter Nicaragua – no way, no how. No amount of pleading, gesticulating, or making fake running movements in the direction of Honduras could dissuade them and we were forced to turn around. We surmised that because we had not officially entered Honduras, we could simply return to Nicaragua, but such was not the case.

It turns out that because we had paid our exit fee, we were essentially in purgatory, four gringos destined to haunt the border region for years to come. Unless, that is, we paid our entrance fee to get back into Nicaragua, the country we had actually never left. And so with heavy hearts – and the knowledge that we would need to attempt another border crossing to Costa Rica within the month – we shelled out another $12 each (to the same lady we had paid our exit fee to), lining the pockets of those that uphold a corrupt immigration system yet ensuring that our taxi driver's wait was over. It was ironic that our mini border debacle happened on the same day Trump announced his frightening major updates to the US immigration policy, making border crossings, for many, not just an inconvenience but an impossibility.

There is a Manny Ramirez, a Mickey Mantle, or a Roberto Clemente waiting around every corner in El Tololar. Really, the kids here can play baseball, possessing the raw talent that in a different world would give many of them access to the big leagues, the *grandas ligas*. But they lack something kind of essential to the game… equipment. Several of our friends and family have been so kind to donate balls and gloves. We gave some to one of the local elementary schools to use. Harlan, at one time or another, has come running to the house mid-game to procure a new ball, having lost the last one in either the pile of peanut leftovers at Don Leonel's or in the cow paddock that abuts the baseball field near the bus stop.

This piecemeal approach to baseball development worked fine for a time, but last week we hit on an even better one. Our neighbor Adilsa (who is literally connected to everyone in the village) brought the local coach in waiting, Paulo, to our house for a chat. Paulo has been wanting to start a baseball team in Tololar, and has great plans for entering the team into local leagues while coaching them to be a legitimate contender. He really thinks he can do it, and now, thanks to donations, he can. It seems small, but Paulo was so happy when he received the assortment of gloves and baseballs. He could envision each glove encircling the hand of a 12-year-old protégé, or a ball careening off the bat of the next big slugger from El Tololar. Bats and balls may seem trivial, but when they get in the right hands, then they are magic.

Running is not a thing in El Tololar. It is just not part of the culture, partly because people here don't have a lot, and free time is spent either working in the fields or looking for work. At the end of a long day toiling under the hot sun, often a nice swing on a hammock is preferable to a lengthy, sweat-filled run. Plus, almost no one can afford a new pair of running shoes. Our good friend Tyler, who is the reason we are here, began running when he worked here from 2008-2010 with the Peace Corps. Tyler, along with local partners, subsequently started Tololamos – www.tololamos.org – with whom we are privileged to continue to partner. Tyler introduced us to his peanut-field route when we arrived, and for the first three months we ran there a few times a week, jumping in between the green peanut plants while we looked up at the smoking volcanoes that stood in the distance.

A couple weeks back we shifted our running route as the peanut field, now all plowed over, has become something of a dustbowl, as has virtually all of El Tololar. Our route takes us on a dirt road (a bit less dusty than the peanut field, unless your run coincides with the daily walking of the cows, in which case it's both dusty, stinky and a bit dangerous), across a peanut field – they are hard to avoid – and along another dirt road that passes the elementary school, the same one Harlan and Olle will attend two days a week starting soon. The route continues past the school and the clinic, and back up through another peanut field to our house. It's approximately four miles round trip.

One day when Cully was running, a young man drove by on a motorcycle. He stopped, clearly concerned, and asked if Cully needed a ride. It was inconceivable that the guy running down the street with a stick (you always run with a branch to shoo dogs away) might actually be running… for exercise, for the fun of it. His look of concern was only equaled in magnitude by the blank, perplexed stares we often get from the cows we pass, similarly baffled by the running aliens. Yet an equally important aspect of the encounter with the moto-ist was that he stopped; he saw someone from a different tribe, a different culture, and a different language, and he crossed the divide to make a connection. In the end, Cully declined the offer of the ride (he really was exercising!), but he was thankful for the motorcycle Samaritan, because the guy did what we should all do: take a chance, a risk, cross the line, and connect with someone different from ourselves.

For the past two months, we've been teaching English, every Tuesday and Thursday afternoon. We've had a mixed group of students, from Harlan and Olle's baseball, hang-out friends, to assorted members of the Rivas family, to local high school students who through word of mouth have heard about the classes. Harlan and Olle have taken a turn or two helping teach (perhaps planting the seed to be future educators?) but generally it's Miriam and Cully who lead the classes. We've done body parts (including belly button – *ombligo*, which is just kind of a funny word), some basic verbs, colors, greetings, the alphabet, and most recently, prepositions. We've taken to teaching the class in both Spanish and English, partly because we feel like we had mixed results in our initial Spanish classes that were ALL in Spanish. Still, we get a fair few looks of bewilderment (it's like we're running), and you realize how difficult learning another language can be. "What on earth are these two talking about", they must think, "and for goodness' sakes why is stomach so hard to pronounce in English." We get it, because we still have many moments of great frustration and confusion with Spanish. But little by little (*poco a poco*) we are getting there, and we hope they are too.

What does an onion cost? Like 25 cents, if that? Here in Nicaragua, an onion costs a few *cordobas*, depending on the size, only cents on the dollar. Most of us wouldn't think twice about shelling that out. But let's shift the analogy. Let's pretend you are a resident of El Tololar. The dry season has kicked into full swing, and for some reason, every day you only have water for a few hours. The spigot runs dry. You and your neighbors put up with this for the better part of a month, but then you've had enough. You come together and set up a meeting with the local water officials to find out what the heck is going on. Hundreds of you congregate one sultry afternoon, and you air your grievances. "I need water to wash clothes, for my animals, to cook, to drink", you all say. The water officials act like they care, yet divulge little but scuttlebutt and empty promises. Then finally they say, "okay, we will release more water, but only if you pay six *cordobas* for 3 meters of water." That's a pittance, right? But then you begin to think of that onion, or that tomato. Not being able to buy one isn't a big deal, but when you add those *cordobas* up over time, it really impacts your bottom line. The price differential could mean missing a meal, or two or three, and that's a problem, because we all need to eat.

So when injustice is happening around us, like an unjust water bill, or something else, we speak up. We see something that is just not right, doesn't add up (for ourselves, or for other people, because heck, we are all in this world together) and we stand up, we unite, because there is strength in numbers. And guess what? The water bill thing worked out. Since that meeting, the water flow has not been perfect, and is never sufficient, but it's been a heck of a lot better. Any why? Thanks to the perseverance and tenacity of people like our friend Adilsa. She led the charge, organized people, and mobilized a strong show of resistance to the water committee's proposed changes; and they couldn't ignore her.

If you ever happen to be driving on Nicaraguan Highway One, about an hour north of Esteli, you need to stop at Somoto Canyon. We hired a local guide, a young, spry lad of about 60 named Anastasio Martinez, to take us through. We walked together with Anastasio, teaching each other our respective mother tongues. His dream, even at sixty (don't you just love someone who never stops dreaming?) is to learn English. He taught us about the local flora and fauna as we walked along a ridge, then down into the canyon. The water was chilly (especially to our bodies that have become accustomed to the really hot El Tololar climate) but the sun made enough appearances over the canyon walls to keep our shivering level to a minimum.

As we walked – and sometimes swam or tubed – we were met on three occasions by jumbo Blue Morpho butterflies, rare but perhaps the most beautiful butterflies you will ever meet. There were other people in the canyon that day, but for the most part, we felt alone, floating together with only the Morphos and the high cliff walls as our companions. Perhaps the highlight of the trip was when Harlan and Olle (their nerves that day were steelier than the water was icy) each launched off a 5-meter high cliff into the narrow but deep, blue gorge below. Olle had never attempted such a leap, and it was awesome to see the initial fear in his eyes give way to a twinkle, and then a huge grin when he came up for air.

From the Desk of Harlan:

> The things I like to do in Nicaragua are playing with Leo, big soccer games, and León days. It is fun to play with Leo (who is a local boy) because I am interacting with another kid my age. I continue to try and find more opportunities to hang out with kids in the community. I also think Leo is cool because we play competition sports like soccer and baseball together. Sometimes I get bored here, but playing with Leo is hours of entertainment. He is a good friend. Big soccer games are great because I can get better at soccer while having fun with the family. I also like them because I can feel like I am speaking to the people fluently in Spanish through sports.
>
> Three reasons I like Nicaragua are, getting to know the culture, the experience and seeing things, and the new things I am learning. For

> getting to know the culture, I get to talk to and get to know and understand the people. We also get to see the poverty especially in our days in León. The best part is we get to learn the language (Spanish). For the experience, we get to go to another country. We also get to learn what they do. We get to go to the school here to interact with other kids. For finding knew things, I have found out passion by being here and feeling what it is like. I found out persistence by staying here for this whole time. I found out experience by seeing everything. These are the things I like about being in Nicaragua.

Three weeks ago we took a trip to the town primary school where some other volunteers from Spain had organized games for the kids. So we walked there with Adilsa (one of the family members we live with, she also works at the school, and she is incredible) and her grandson Leo. When we got there, the outside space near the library was full of kids and games. Olle, Leo, and I stood on the side not really interested in any of the puzzles or board games. Then some twenty minutes later the running games started and the kids at the school were having the time of their lives. It was a really cool experience. It was really fun mainly for the kids here because they never get access to games like that. It was very interesting to see what it was like. It affected me because in the United States we take stuff like that for granted and don't appreciate it as much.

Chapter 14:
Catastrophes, Dust in the Wind, Secret Gardens

Early/Mid-February

We had just boarded the bus from El Tololar to León, and it was early, 4:30 a.m. A few women were already seated, scattered the length of the Bluebird Bus, no doubt heading to work as cooks or food sellers in one of León's four main markets. All the local buses in Nicaragua are either of the Bluebird, LaidLaw or Thomas variety – the three main school bus companies in the US – and it's entirely possible that one of you rode this very bus as a child in the states – most of the buses here are at least thirty or forty years old. But then it would have looked very different, having since been transformed by the addition of bright reds, whites, and greens with black accents.

Forty years ago it wouldn't have had spiritual quotes splashed on its front and sides, such as John 14:6 – "No one comes to the Father except through me." It wouldn't have had a sign on the back that read, "*siempre listo*" (always ready), but it likely still would have featured the same English signs up front, indicating a 'Drug Free School Zone' and noting that 'Your children's safety is our business.' The buses' insides would have looked similar, but without luggage racks running the length of either side, made to hold the various bags of rice, beans, sugar, baskets of vegetables, slats of aluminum, and the occasional chicken.

The seats would have been related, albeit with less rips and scratch marks, but back then you would not have been able to see the bumpy, rocky, dusty, dirt road through various rusted-out view holes in the floor. But some of the universal school bus riding rules would apply in both situations, such as always check to make sure you don't sit in the row three-quarters of the way back, the row with the wheel hump, because even more so than when you were a kid, space on a chicken bus in Nicaragua is at a premium.

When you were a kid, the bus would have driven down largely paved roads, possibly with the occasional rural dirt road mixed in for good measure. You would have ridden only with your fellow students, not with the smorgasbord of night watchmen, cooks, farmers, teachers, students and day laborers that are your riding partners here. Your ride would have been free, not 11 or 12 *cordobas*, but you would have missed the experience of watching the *cobradors* in action, the money-takers who manage to calculate and give change on the fly, bobbing and weaving through assorted legs, arms, bags, and body parts as they make their way towards the rear of the bus.

You would likely not have seen volcanoes in the distance as you rode your bus to elementary school, and you would not have had to stop every half mile to let a bike down from the roof, or unload a sack of yucca through the rear. You certainly would not have been able to listen to the peddlers who jump on and off the bus, selling health products that promise to cure every ailment from indigestion to cancer, or listen to the blind man sing an out of tune song that's worth every coin you can find in your pocket. Women would not have handed you, a total stranger, their two-month old child to hold and love while they searched for their fare. Two boys, one the mouthpiece for the other, would not have boarded, holding giant photos of boy #2 naked in front of you, with a catheter and clearly suffering from some severe condition.

Your bus's engine would still have been relatively new, so you would have missed the grinding, chalk-boardy sounds created every time the driver shifted to a new gear. Machetes would not have been allowed on your bus, and so you would have missed the sound of hacking and chopping as the *ayudante* (assistant) leaned out from time to time to chop a low-hanging tree, preparing the way for a rare but amazing sight – the passing of two school buses (each 8 feet wide) on a road that measures 15ft, 11½ inches.

Every day, it seems, Harlan or Olle say something that just cracks us up. Last week, for example, on our way back from the local primary school, we ran into a man riding a horse and carrying a long, very straight piece of wood, from the looks of it a piece of eucalyptus. We said hi, and asked what he was using the wood for, remarking on its excellent straightness. He responded that it was to be used for building a house. A little ways down the road, Olle quipped, "Is he really going to build a whole house with just that piece of wood?" Harlan was sick recently, another day to join his personal parade of different types of ailments, seemingly coming one after the other with literally no stop since we arrived. As he returned from the third of many visits to the John, he said definitively, "The only good thing that came from today is that my wart fell off!" Now there is something we can build on.

We came home from León the other day and upon entering our room, Miriam mentioned there was a rather large lizard under our roof. Roof is a fluid concept here, and the lizard was in fact both under our roof, and sort of on our wall, as there is a large space in between the two. The lizard was not just rather large, but a certifiable iguana, close to 2 feet long with tail, and looking far too comfortable as it nonchalantly looked down on us. We tried the broom-shoo-away trick, which didn't do much, and then decided to leave her there, figuring maybe iguanas also ate mice, who have also set up shop near our roof. We haven't seen Lizzy since.

We recently had a really strange experience that lasted from one night until the next morning. It was one of those stretches of time that is generally explained by either some rare cosmic event like a comet (there wasn't one), or a full moon (which it wasn't). Monday night we had gone to bed a bit out of sorts, as we had not been able to find our rabbit Rainer to put him in the kitchen before bed. We heard a few noises during the night – dog-like noises – and checked a time or two to see if Rainer had returned, but we saw hide nor hare of him. Arising to do exercises just before dawn the next day, Rainer was thankfully there, munching weeds outside the kitchen. Our cat Dulce had also returned from a night of wandering as usual, and she purred and rubbed against our legs as we did Pilates (Miriam) and tried to touch our toes (Cully). Not five minutes later, all hell broke loose, ending in tragedy.

Cully was just starting a set of exercises when Dulce, who we had seen purring contently only five minutes before, came running back from the brush, making a strange gargling noise as she careened into our bedroom. It was still partially dark, and at first we thought she might have caught a mouse or strange animal. We entered the bedroom to a chilling sight. Dulce was writhing in pain, partially foaming at the mouth, and slamming her body against the wall. Our first thought was of course rabies, and we stayed our distance, but also remembered that animals in the whole area had been vaccinated for rabies and there hadn't been a case in some time. Dulce's writhing slowed and as Cully ran to get our neighbor Adilsa, her breathing slowed even more. By the time they returned, Dulce was just barely moving, laying in front of Miriam at the foot of our bed on the concrete floor. Less than 10 minutes from when she ran into the room, she was dead.

Dulce's death was hard on all of us for a lot of reasons, partly because she was the first pet we acquired once we arrived and she possessed a great temperament, always ready to snuggle, and purr, and comfort when one of us needed. The next day we dug a hole in our backyard with Don Leonel's help, lowering Dulce's body in a shopping bag while Harlan and Olle took turns covering her with dirt. Buried with Dulce was a note from Olle that read, "Farewell, Gatita (Spanish name for female kitten), May Your Spirit Linger On, Queen of Gatitas." The working theory by most people here was that Dulce was stung by a large *alacron* (scorpion) and that the poison was just too much for her small body. Others think it could have been a really rare but highly venomous coral snake. It is crazy how sometimes life and death are not that far apart.

Community health in rural communities all around the world probably doesn't look that much different from one village to the next. Sure there are cultural distinctions, varying degrees of human and financial resources at one's disposal, differing climates, and assorted health issues specific to each region. But boots on the ground is a constant element; the health workers at times need to go directly to people's houses, to both care for the sick and to obtain vital demographic information.

Olle and Cully had the chance to accompany several of El Tololar's health workers, including *La Doctora* Maria, to the community last week on an information gathering outing. At each house, the doctor would begin with greetings, and then quickly move to questions. "How many people are at home today? How many people live here? How many children? What are their ages? Has anyone's family member died recently? Are any of the women pregnant? How many months? How many of the women have had pap smears? When and where did they have them?" The doctor fired off her questions, sometimes having to wait longer than you would expect for answers. She would ask other personal questions as well, building trust while obtaining valuable data for census purposes, but also to improve the health outcomes in El Tololar.

The doctor put small packets of little crystals in any standing barrel of water she found in order to kill mosquito larvae (they do a great job; we have seen minimal mosquitoes since we arrived). She also provided each family member with anti-parasite pills, that she strongly urged them to take. This personalized house-to-house approach to preventative healthcare is so different from what we have in the US, and while it is really draining and exhausting to walk through dust, dung and sun, it can and does save lives. Next month our whole family (Miriam was caring for a sick Harlan on this expedition) hopes to join the doctor once again to watch her in action: hearing and helping and healing.

We generally shun dust, for good reason. First of all, it's just plain dusty; it's dirty, it makes you sneeze and cough, and it gets in your eyes, nose and in between every toe. Plus, it has a way of covering everything with a fine, thin layer, from the top of your coffee maker, to your makeshift kitchen table, to your motley assortment of pots and pans. When it's windy, it flies through the air, creating dust devils and mini-tornadoes.

Our friends here told us of a time when they had to adopt a special dust-preventative method for eating tortillas; as soon as the wind showed signs of letting up, they would eat really quickly, hoping to swallow them before the dust could mix in and create an unwanted 'sandwich'.

But there is a flip-side to dust, if you care to explore it, a beautiful side. There are times, rare times, in the lazy, waning afternoon, when it mixes with falling but fading sun to create dancing beams of light, giving everything in its path a heavenly glow. If you sit in just the right spot later that same day, now at dusk, at times the dust – again with its partner the sun – will bend through the slots in the makeshift fresco that sits above your bedroom door, mingling with the shadows of twisted palm leaves as it makes its journey to the floor. Most things, even particulate matter, can have an upside. But to be real, the dust here just plain sucks.

If you were a used pair of sneakers or sandals, or perhaps a dress shirt, or a nice pair of pants, what would you want to do when your life of regular usage was over? Would you like to sit in a box, gathering dust, destined to deteriorate and smell like moth balls for the rest of your life, until the day you were either finally pitched into the garbage, or possibly burnt in the backyard along with assorted trash, fallen maple and oak leaves, and the remains of trees? No, you would want to live in the light of day, you'd want to be useful. And if you happened to be the traveling type, you'd want to see the world, and explore a new culture, wouldn't you? Well thanks to a recent shipment from some pretty awesome family members, an assortment of clothes are getting their wish, and making people extremely happy in the process.

When Chepe – an exceedingly gentle but reclusive guy – recently received his new sandals, for example, he broke into the biggest smile we've seen on him since we arrived. Aquiles couldn't hide his pleasure when a new dress shirt appeared at his door, definitely the first new, high quality shirt he'd come across in years. And Adilsa, a woman who is always, always, giving to others, upon receiving her new blouse, expressed her gratitude by promptly wearing it… every day! Used clothes are no more than an afterthought for many of us. For people in El Tololar, they make a big difference, as the typical person's wardrobe here consists of a couple t-shirts and pants, one dress outfit (but with stains and rips from too many barbed-wire fence drying sessions), a couple changes of underwear and socks, and a pair of shorts or two, in most cases zipperless, buttonless, holy shorts that have no business on a body. Clothes, including used ones, bring smiles and grins.

Trees, glorious, trees, are a lot of hard work. Several years ago, Tololamos started a planting project to address the problems that climate change (less water) and peanuts (more dust, more health issues) have wrought in El Tololar. The project's goal is to help mitigate the dust and erosion problems that are a huge part of life here – and by extension improve health outcomes – by providing people access to tree saplings which can serve as windbreaks and dust barriers, shade-makers that increase soil retention. Despite the usual challenges of operating in Nicaragua, the project has seen some great success, and this year looks as promising as ever.

Our family had the chance to participate in the planting project on a few mornings and we gained a new respect for what it takes. Are you ready?

1. Identify better location for nursery than last time when iguanas ate the saplings
2. Buy planting bags

3. Hire workers
4. Fill at least 6,000 bags with soil (dirty, dusty, ibuprofen-inducing work even if you only fill a relative few like we did)
5. Procure seeds that are the right type for this climate and community
6. Buy tools like wheelbarrows and chicken wire for fence
7. Plant seeds in bags
8. Water 6,000 bags several times a day
9. Wait a few months till seeds turn to saplings
10. Advertise
11. Supply seeds to community members
12. Give instructions on how to care
13. Pray for rain.

It's a lot of work, and a fair bit of risk, but the difference made, over time, is big.

Ready for school? Miriam has been homeschooling Harlan and Olle since we arrived. It's not easy, to say the least. But she and the boys are doing an awesome job, in spite of having to teach and learn in a really difficult operating environment. To augment the boys' Spanish and their connection to kids in the community, on Monday they started attending the local elementary school, Rebekah Rivas. We bought their uniforms (white shirt, blue pants), filled their backpacks with supplies, gave them a few extra *cordobas* to get a snack, and headed to school, a 40-minute walk through peanut fields and paths, past barking dogs, crowing roosters, and herds of cows.

We arrived late, and the students were already all in line, receiving the week's instructions. We were promptly ushered up to the front, where a teacher named Samir graciously introduced our family and let the students know that two days a week, Harlan and Olle would be joining the sixth and fourth grades respectively. We then lip-synched the national anthem, met their teachers, and then they were whisked off to their respective classrooms. At first Harlan didn't have a desk to sit at, but no worries. The students found an old broken desk out behind the school and fixed it, post haste. It is not easy to just enter a new class, in a different country, using a new language, and we will see how the experiment pans out. But we are so proud of both the boys after just the first two days, being game to take a risk, stepping outside their comfort zones (a term that has gotten a real workout this year for our family) and trusting in their own abilities, and the goodness of others.

There are many ways to get bad second degree burns, none of which are fun. Take the following two examples. Miriam awoke early on Tuesday (3:20 a.m.) to take part in a ritual that women all over El Tololar engage in every morning… making food. Some women (come on guys, let's start cooking too) make food for their families, and others for sale. In the case of our friend Ivania, the one we helped purchase a horse,she cooks food to sell at the local primary and secondary schools. Harlan and Olle are actually two of her best customers. Miriam arrived just before 4am, having avoided multiple close encounters in the dark with a variety of snappy, feisty dogs – including a really big, scary, black dog that none of us like (think Cujo) – and promptly began helping Ivania make *enchiladitos*, yucca chips, and freshly-squeezed juice. They cooked in the smoky, partially open-air kitchen and had a great time connecting while preparing food for many of El Tololar's students.

After cooking, Miriam turned her attention to planting for a time, again helping fill the bags with soil for the Tololamos reforestation project. She finished a little late, but was offered a motorcycle ride to the bus stop. Upon disembarking, her calf came into contact with the muffler (hello, why are these not protected?), giving her a really bad, painful burn that will leave a mark, to say the least. We also heard that Rosibel, our former Spanish teacher, received a really bad burn on her backside last week while watching a firework show (fireworks here are generally not that colorful or brilliant, but rather opt for loud noise and peril as their main selling points).

There is a quote that says "*León es la ciudad que esta cerrado afuera y abierto adentro*" (León is the city that is closed on the outside but open on the inside). We've found this to be true. Walking down the streets, León can at times seem somewhat plain, with not a lot of commercial or private activity. There are simple storefronts with unimpressive facades and except for the fifteen or so beautiful historic churches scattered around the city, it can be pretty unremarkable in places. That is until you go inside. There you will find beautiful courtyards, green spaces, gorgeous birds, butterflies, and an array of flowers that would make many arboretum curator blush. These spaces exist as living secrets, and only those who have a key or are invited in get to share in their abundance. In many ways, we too are often like these secret gardens; we have so much to give and share, but only those who have the key or dare to enter in can truly see our souls.

Chapter 15:

Making Out with Strangers, Maria Jerez, Sex Education

Late February/Early March

Pulperias are stores, often tiny ones that sell all sorts of things you might need in a pinch: ice, eggs, rice, beans, soda, hammocks, cheese, milk. They are like mini-marts, but usually operate out of someone's house, like a *venta*, and so you get the bonus of buying your victuals while saying hi to grandma in the nearby rocking chair, "*Buenos Dias, Abuela!*", or seeing a lone teenager at the back of the store working on his homework assignment in the fading afternoon light. On a recent run by *Pulperia* Stefany, a small beach-side shop not too far from our house, a serious logging procedure was underway.

In fact, it was a de-logging operation as ten men were cutting down a tree that was growing out of the middle of Stefany. Who knows why the little market allowed a tree to remain in her midst for so long -perhaps the owners just liked trees – but clearly the time had come to cut it out. And so the men chopped, cut, pulled and lowered, using big tools and a lot of teamwork. Watching the activity going down that morning brought a thought to mind; we are sometimes like Stefany. Little things start to grow inside us, like tendencies, insecurities, anger, or fear. We let them grow because they're small and we think we know how to manage them. But they get bigger and bigger, and soon grow through the roof, breaking things and shattering our sense of self in the process. But we continue to let them stay, because now removing them is a lot of hard work and energy, and besides, it requires the help of others – and we just don't like to ask others for help. But imagine if we could live without the tree through our roof, the hole in our heart, or the pain in our soul. Imagine if we could enlist the help of friends, some sweat equity, and a lot of hard work, to uproot the trees that hold us back in life. Thanks for the lesson, Stefany.

Transitioning to a new environment can be hard. We recently spent almost two weeks at the beach near our house with some really awesome friends (thanks Anthony family, Mardi, Chris and Jen). They blessed us, pampered us, and cooked some truly exquisite food. We will never be able to thank them enough. But the beach environs were so different than our house in the village that at first the change was a bit jarring, but in a good way. "You mean there aren't any tarantulas here, really?" We said. "We don't have to wash our laundry by hand?" "We'll be eating more than just rice and beans. Do you really mean it?"

The whole experience was marvelous, and perhaps there was only one element that reminded us of our home in El Tololar. Cully and Miriam woke up on successive nights in their gorgeous bedroom overlooking the Pacific Ocean. They each heard some squeaking and scurrying, all too familiar sounds that could mean only one thing… ratones!… but where? Confounded, they looked up at a star-lit shadow on the wall. If you've never seen it, the apparition of mice marching to the light of the night, when projected in just the right way, can be really scary, particularly because the tiny mice look like giant, man-eating rats. We never found the mice, just their shadows, but a plethora of poops on the porch confirmed it wasn't a dream.

The reverse transition, from beautiful ocean-view to hot, dusty village life is also difficult. Upon returning from our stint at the beach we were welcomed by a slew of new friends that had taken up residence in various quiet corners, dark places, and hard to reach nooks in our house. We awoke a sizable scorpion when opening our kitchen window and whacked another hiding underneath a suitcase in Harlan and Olle's room. Miriam encountered a good size mouse near the suitcase scorpion, and not long after a large tarantula on the wall near our pee bucket. Some giant feces were also sitting on top of our mosquito net, an indication that the iguana we had previously seen under our roof was likely still there. Lots and lots of dust from two weeks of blowing wind needed to be swept out (we have found it's hard to sweep dust with any efficacy while the wind is blowing), and cobwebs in our rafters and bugs in our clothes required removal. The considerable cleaning operation, plus the realization that we were back to a life full of wind and dust, and lacking in water, gave us a moment to consider our local friends and neighbors, who have to deal with these situations every day and every season.

We continue to make lots of mistakes in our Spanish, like last week when Cully explained to Adilsa that it was possible that his rabbit, a well-respected veterinarian, might come to help castrate cows and bulls; the words for brother-in-law (*cuñado*) and rabbit (*conejo*) are not that far off in Spanish. Another time, we confirmed that a meeting should occur next egg if not before (*Jueves* and *huevos* are alike, aren't they?).

PO boxes are very useful when you are living overseas. In fact, since we've been here we've received all sorts of packages and goodies from friends and family back home, all addressed to: Familia Lundgren, Apártado 324, León, Nicaragua, Central America. Most boxes have actually arrived, albeit with travel times ranging from 1 and a half weeks to two months. Recently, that may have changed, at least for a moment, with the curious case of the disappearing post office. On one of our weekly trips to León, Cully stopped by the post office to check on the latest arrivals. He was greeted by an almost entirely empty building only occupied by several women sweeping and washing the floors.

It turns out the post office had up and moved without notice, pushed out by the rather angry owner of the premises who seemed miffed by the deterioration that had occurred to her rental property over the many years of occupancy by the PO. She kindly directed Cully to the new location, located four blocks east and 1 and a half blocks north, where Cully promptly encountered several rather disoriented looking workers, clearly out of place in the new, much tinier environs. The woman who gives us our mail, known as the 'package lady' to the Lundgrens, was at the bank and no one knew when she would be back. Perhaps more disconcerting was that PO Box 324 was not among the wooden boxes that had been stacked rather haphazardly near the entrance. It seems that in the hurried move, 324 had gone on a walkabout and had yet to return. A second trip to the León PO by Familia Lundgren didn't produce any better results, and we can only hope that someday soon, when ol' 324 has had enough sightseeing, she'll return to her new address.

Our chickens are growing up quickly, fueled by a daily diet of *semillas de trigo* (wheat seeds), cooked rice, insects and spiders. Our chickens are also getting tough, because they have to fight the dogs, other chickens, and our bunny, all whom try to eat their food every time we cast it on the ground near their coop. As they've grown, they've also taken to roosting on one of the three eucalyptus beams that span the top of our patio. In general the new beam-roosting technique is great, except when they choose the beam that sits above our mini dinner table (measuring 28 inches long x 18 inches wide, and standing 2 feet high) as that inevitably results in playing musical-meal-chairs to avoid the intermittent droppings.

"That dog just peed on our clothes," quipped Miriam one morning as a dog sulked away from our clothesline after marking his property. "Was it Sally or Fuera?" asked Cully. "No, it was one of Esteban's dogs," replied Harlan. "Then he's going down," said Cully, as he reached for his trusty slingshot, used to scare away a variety of animals, mostly dogs and nosy chickens, on a frequent basis. "No, I like that dog, he's a good one," said Harlan. "I don't care who he is," answered Cully. "He can't be peeing on our clothes." Harlan's further imploring did little to deter Cully, who launched a rock in the dog's general direction, missing wildly as usual and likely only emboldening the dog for future apparel peeing sessions.

We recently attended a mass at the local Catholic Church, the fourth such service we've attended since we arrived. This one was the one year memorial service for Rosa, the wife of Mariano, our favorite driver of the green and white 6:55am bus from El Tololar to León. Memorial services are common here, and generally follow the same program: start 30-45 minutes late, women sit in pews while men stand idly in the rear, sermon by the always sweaty priest that can't be heard, the casual appearance of bats, snakes or dogs in the sanctuary, and several worship songs with a somewhat out of place zydeco beat.

This service was enhanced further by its occurrence in the middle of the dry, windy season, thus accompanied by loud, beam creaking gusts and waves of dust entering the church through the long, open windows on either side. Congregants generally dress to the hilt, even if it's not on a Sunday, and it's always surprising to see how people can look so beautiful and put together when their reality is dust, dust, dust. At the end of the service, it is customary to go up front and pass on condolences to the family members. Our good friends Kelly and Imran Arshad from Canada were visiting us at the time, and several of us walked up front to pay our respects to Rosa. Nicaraguans are so gentle, kind, and accepting that it seemed totally normal for us to walk past a line of nine sitting women who we didn't know while hugging and kissing each one on the cheek. They accepted the actions of strangers, even if we weren't necessarily following local protocol, genuinely receiving our awkward embraces and ill-timed kisses in a mutual gesture of humanity and connection. They made us feel a part of their community.

But sometimes, especially when you're meeting Dona Maria Jerez for the first time, hugs aren't met with quite so much openness. Cully and his *amigo* Imran (from Canada) had dropped the kids and wives off at Rebekah Rivas Elementary, where the Lundgren and Arshad children were attending school one Monday morning. They walked to a nearby, somewhat dilapidated house where 97-year-old Maria Jerez was said to live. In fact, the Lundgrens had passed by her house previously but only her son had been home. For some reason, he reminded Cully of his own cousin Randy, who lives far away in Vermont. You know how that happens sometimes? Two people, from totally different contexts and worlds, remind you of each other? Sometimes it's because of their looks, but it's more often because of their souls. Randy has a really good soul, and so did Maria's son.

This time, Maria was at home, sitting in a chair with a walker in front of her. Her son (never did get his name, we'll call him Antonio) ushered us in, and Cully quickly walked over to *Senorita* Jerez. After the church hugging/kissing experience from a few days before, he felt confident that giving a big hug and smooch at first greeting was the way to go. But upon leaning in, Maria pushed away and was having none of it. She quickly explained that it was not her custom, partly because she didn't grow up that way, but also because she was mostly blind (cataracts) and couldn't see who this embracing/smacking stranger was.

After the initial shock Maria warmed to us, especially to Imran, who she asked to repeat her name at least four separate times. Imran has always been good at languages and even though he had been in Nicaragua for less than a week, his vocalization of Maria Jerez clearly rolled off his tongue and pleased Maria, who kept saying that Imran's pronunciation was far superior to Cully's. Antonio confirmed the high caliber of Imran's Spanish, as did her nephew Santos, who was sitting off to the side, chain-smoking and drinking a local moonshine at 10am in the morning. They talked for a good twenty minutes, with Maria either reminiscing about the good old days or dismissing Santos with a wave of her cane every time he made an inebriated wisecrack.

The conversation then shifted to the actual purpose of their visit… *jicaro* carvings. Until her eyesight had deteriorated sharply over the past couple years, Maria had been an exquisite carver and artist of *jicaro*, a strange, hard, green fruit that can't be eaten but can look absolutely beautiful as a bowl, a cup, a spoon, or even a Christmas ornament. Maria asked Antonio to open up several bags of her past work, scattering the now dusty but ornately carved tableware, each piece replete with intricately etched lines, leaves and flowers. Before we left, Maria felt the need to show us how she worked and despite Antonio's reticence, he set her up with a freshly picked *jicaro* fruit, a file and a machete.

Watching a nearly blind, 97-year-old woman work a piece of fruit on her lap with a dull blade and shaking hands is scary stuff, but Maria worked it like a boss, demonstrating her still in-tact artistic skills by engraving a beautiful *flor* (flower) and *hoja* (leaf) on the fruit side. She erupted into tears several times, generally when speaking about her grandson who never visited her or her husband who had died four years earlier. She always ended with the phrase, "But thanks be to God." Imran purchased some of her art; she threw in a few spoons as gifts, and we left to her saying thank you and reciting the phrase, "It's just me, a 97-year-old woman and my four *frijoles*." We never quite caught the significance of her four beans…

Our awesome friend Tyler, Executive Director of Tololamos, once taught sex education classes here at the local secondary school. Way to go Tyler. Our boys are learning about the birds and the bees in a slightly different way, through the *Wild Kingdom* (remember that show?) technique. It's not part of the curriculum Miriam is teaching them for school, but Harlan and Olle are nonetheless taking class, daily. Chickens and roosters have been the most consistent teachers, supported by the occasional cow or horse coupling, but recently dogs have stolen the show, thanks largely to Adilsa's dog Sally going into heat. Not less than five local guy dogs have begun to seek out Sally, with Fuera (her best friend) has even received a name change in the process on account of his sexual exploits; sorry Humpy! Poor Sally spends most of her time running away from Humpy, but because she is such a people-dog and always hanging out near us, we often have to shift our views during conversations with family members. Adilsa even rolled her eyes during a recent meeting, noting that freshly-monikered Humpy was in definitely in love, but that Sally clearly wasn't.

The visit by Imran, Kelley, Sage, Xavier and Jai Arshad has marked the fifth group of people that have visited us from North America since we've been here (Miriam's parents, the Anthony Family, the Deleonardis, Mardi Fuller, and the Arshads). One of our goals when we came was to share our story and the community of El Tololar with our friends and families back home. Writing about our experiences is one vehicle, and visits by family and friends is another. Each person that has visited us has been a huge blessing in their own way, sharing themselves and seeing the hearts of the people that we love here. Thank you all so much, and thanks to each and every one of you who is following our journey. Sometimes, many times, we feel like people back home are here with us, sharing a plate of rice and beans.

Chapter 16:
JAWS, Roadside Jesus, Doggie-Paddling

Mid/Late March

Driving home from dropping our good friends off at the airport in Managua, we stopped at a little *Comedor* – basically a small, street-side restaurant that serves up plates of chicken, rice and beans, with the occasional entree option of beef or pork. We were all pretty famished and the heaping plates not only looked good but were tasty, rating pretty high on our local food barometer. We'll give it three out of four *estrellas* (stars). Prior to eating, we asked where the bathroom was and were ushered in through a small door connected to the restaurant. The bathroom was tiny, and strangely situated in the corner of what looked like both a garage and a church worship hall. There was a station wagon, hearse-type vehicle in front of the bathroom, and the rest of the long, narrow room was filled with white fold-up chairs, a makeshift altar and a bathtub that must have been for baptisms.

In Nicaragua there exists such a fluidity and connection between all sorts of spaces. Back home it seems that the boundaries between places and properties are delineated much more clearly, but also more rigidly. Here, for example, the inside of your house is not so removed from your front yard, a restaurant and a church can almost be one in the same, and the place you buy your food staples might be the front living room of someone's house. There's something inviting and welcoming about this approach to living with others that resists being defined or limited, something that is not readily measurable. It seems to say, "Come on in and let's talk and get to know each other without bringing our preconceived baggage, because guess what, yes this is my house, but it's also my restaurant, my business, and the place I worship. I am many things, and have many layers and so do you, so let's get to know each other. Welcome!"

Volcanoes evoke power and strength while inspiring fear and trepidation. But usually they are far away from us, standing only as silent witnesses and seers to the devastation they once wrought and reminders of the destruction they might unleash again at any time. They are also creative forces, breaking down and building up, covering and then unearthing. Nicaragua has something like twenty-six volcanoes, a good portion of which are considered active, including Telica and San Cristobal – the country's largest mountain at 1,754 meters – both of which are always watching us when we walk to school, run in the peanut field, or ride the bus to León.

Masaya is both the name of a small city south of the capital Managua and of a large volcano, one of the more active ones in Nicaragua. It is so active, in fact, that you can actually look down into the enormous crater and see red hot lava, spurting, frothing and looking every bit as mean as you would expect thousand some-odd degree lava to look. Either because it's so spectacular (or possibly so dangerous) each vehicle that drives up the mountain gets five – count em five – minutes to explore the crater's rim.

We drove up at just past 4:30 p.m., passing a panorama of volcanic rock and magma residue from previous eruptions, nine of us spilling out of our absurdly large micro-bus rental (the only size that would fit our party was a 16-passenger Toyota Hiace) as we raced to make the most of our *cinco minutos* of viewing time. Approaching the rim we peered over the fence, expecting a rush of red liquid to engulf us and our van, Pompeii-style. Instead we were greeted by a gorgeous crater and farther in, deeper into its gut, we saw lava – real, live lava. It was a pretty special experience, and it was a true bummer when the park guard/stopwatch lady began waving her hands that our time was up. But it's all good because now, we're all lava whisperers.

"We might see Jesus on our walk home," remarked Cully as we left our friend Ivania's house after having dropped off some donated clothes that many family and friends were kind enough to send. In fact we had seen Jesus on our walk to Ivania's, replete with a crown of thorns, a purple robe, and of course a cross. He had been standing idly under the porch of one of our neighbors, surrounded by cows, waiting to begin his march to the church. We caught up with him almost in front of Yader's house, now being carried by four strong men (including Yader and Fernando). A woman was standing in front of Jesus reading some words we couldn't hear, and as the small procession of thirty or so people passed us, we saw the afternoon light shining down and reflecting off the cross.

All along the dirt road, people were sweeping and raking garbage and leaves and then burning them, cleaning the road for the procession and leaving a dry, earthly fragrance in their wake. Others were setting up chairs and throwing water on the road so that Jesus and his bearers could stay semi dust-free. The procession continued past us, a small but committed band of followers, proving very adept at dodging oncoming trucks (two), motorcycles (three) and a herd of cows (forty). Their walk to the church was hot and dusty and not without obstacles, but they persevered with a faith you could sense but not see. We are told the same parade plays itself out every

Friday during Lent at about 4 p.m. up until Easter, and there is a good shot we'll see the *Via Crucis* play out again.

Lake Nicaragua is the largest body of water in Central America and depending on your viewpoint, it can look like a real ocean, at times even sporting mini-waves that you could almost ride. It spans much of the southern part of the country, and has all sorts of cool places to hike, swim, kayak, and just chillax. The city of Granada (one of the oldest colonial cities in Central America) sits on the lake's shore and it's not hard to find a guide who will take you on a tour of *Las Isletas*, some 365 small islands that stretch out from Granada's shores in a mini-archipelago. Most of the islands are tiny but what they lack in size they make up in panoramic excellence as they are framed by the gorgeous lake and cool sounding volcanoes like *Mombacho*.

Lots of the islands are home to Nicaragua's rich and famous (there are a quite a few of them, including the Pellas family who has interests in the national beer (Toña) and the national rum (Flor de Caña)) and you can meander through and among the islands on a motorboat or by kayak. We took the motorized option for a one-and-a-half-hour tour which we were pretty happy about, especially after we found that the lake, known locally as *Cocibolca,* is home to the Lake Nicaragua Shark, a relative of the saltwater bull shark. This crazy fish has figured out a way to leave the ocean, swim up a nearby river and literally 'leap' into the lake. They get up to five meters in length, and are considered one of the more aggressive types of sharks. AND THEY'RE IN A LAKE! But for anyone coming to visit, don't worry, there have been very few attacks… so far.

In December, a new handmade bed arrived in our front yard, hauled by Yader, Fernando, and a horse. The same trio delivered a new dining room (our open-air patio) table a couple weeks back, but this time out of the blue. Like, who does that? Just delivers a new table to your house, unannounced and ready to eat off? The Valdivia family, that's who. Perhaps they realized our need when we had them over for dinner in January and attempted to fit eight people around our dinky coffee table. Or it may have been during one of our monthly movie nights, when they marveled how our little *mesa* (table) could balance four 3-liter bottles of black, red (the nasty stuff), orange and green sodas, ten bowls of popcorn, and a DVD player. Either way, the freshly delivered table, made by Yader's dad Yader, is massive in comparison, handcrafted out of black pine and currently used to eat, play cards, fold clothes, and study on. Now our problem is our chairs, which in comparison to the table make our entire family look like little munchkins when we eat.

It only seems fitting that our most recent injury happened to Harlan, who severely jammed his left index finger while wave riding at Poneloya Beach. We think his finger rammed into his brother Olle's hip, as if Harlan was pointing at Olle to move aside to allow for a smooth ride to shore. Miriam splinted it with a popsicle-stick device, but given its location near his growth plate, we decided to seek a doctor's advice. Miriam and Harlan's medical consult adventure involved making a series of appointments with multiple doctors and offices.

The first clinic they tried had no orthopedic doctors on hand, while the second they found only by chance after receiving three sets of conflicting directions. There they made an appointment with Doctor Rafael Cruz for the next day at the Ruben Dario Clinic (Dario, a poet, is given almost saint-like status in Nicaragua), but in the meantime followed a lead to the *Centro de Imágenes Diagnósticas San Sebastian* where they were told they could get the finger x-rayed. Unfortunately, prior to x-rays they were required to actually have a medical consult and thus had to leave the deliciously air-conned office, cross the street, and wait for one hour to be seen by Dr. Carlos Lopez.

After a quick examination of the digit, Miriam and Harlan re-crossed the road to get the x-ray. The chickens then crossed the road again to get to the other side and have the x-rays read by Dr. Lopez, who initially diagnosed a break, then re-re-referred them to yet another doctor who was said to be equipped with the proper casting materials. They were at this point almost done, only needing to pay for the third time, visit another doctor's office across town where the diagnosis was changed from break to jam, and pay for the fourth time in three hours – easy-peasy. In the end, Harlan's finger could be found wrapped securely in the popsicle-stick device, gauzed and taped, exactly as Miriam had dressed it in the first place. But on the up side, Miriam and Harlan were successful in virtually geo-mapping every orthopedic-related office in the Greater León area in record time.

One Sunday morning, we had a cow break. The usual early rising animal suspects are our cat, rabbit, two juvenile chickens, Adilsa's two dogs, Don Leonel's two or three horses, Miriam and Carlos's five pigs, the occasional errant rooster, a once in a while wild skunk, and one or more of our neighbor Esteban's nettlesome dogs. But bovines never swing by our house. On this particular day, we were holding school at our home, rare for a Sunday but necessary in order to catch the boys up with the copious amounts of school they had missed (they weren't complaining!) during consecutive visits by beloved friends. We noticed a cow grazing nearby, and didn't think much of it until Carlos came through our patio, shooing it away. Whatever it was munching was clearly off limits. Next Aquiles came by, tossing rocks and using a stick to motivate her to mooove on. He did this twice, and then Harlan and Cully, in the middle of Chapter 30, Unit 4 of Math Class – Solving One-Step, Real World Problems – decided to put their learning to the test.

Harlan grabbed a broom and Cully a couple rocks. Using a team approach, they came at her from opposite sides, the wildly waving broom and flying rock combo doing the trick initially. She came back four more times during math class, twice with the intention of eating Adilsa's nearby nascent banana plants, and each time she left for five minutes before returning. Only when Adilsa returned on her motorcycle and brought down the hammer (don't mess with Adilsa when a cow is eating her garden) did Bessie move on for good.

We used to like dogs… really. In fact, prior to coming to Nicaragua, we liked them a lot. Both Miriam and Cully had dogs as pets growing up, and still have fond memories of playing fetch, being met at the door by a wagging, slobbery friend, or going on long walks with a faithful companion by your side. Things have changed for a couple reasons. First, dogs are literally everywhere in El Tololar. They are usually scrawny, not well cared for, and pretty stinky. They're scrawny because they are lucky even to get leftover table scraps, and thus are always scrounging for food. This means that on any given day, five to ten different dogs are lurking at the edges of our yard, waiting for the right opportunity to make a dive into our garbage pit, where admittedly they could probably find some pretty good chow. We still try to shoo them away when we can, but it's tiring grabbing a slingshot and a rock every half hour, so they often have free reign in our hole.

Existing in a constant state of starvation also makes them desperate, and often downright mean. About 1 a.m. on a recent full moon night, Cully awoke to hear a *whole lotta shaking going* on in the kitchen. Rainer our rabbit had thankfully slept outside under Aquiles' latrine that night as he is wont to do, so the kitchen commotion was all the more perplexing as we were sure (pretty sure) we had locked our kitchen door. Not. Upon opening our bedroom door, two of Esteban's dogs (oh, how we loathe them) sprinted out of our kitchen with either very guilty looks or sly grins, fortunately only having eaten six eggs. Doggy desperation for food also leads to aggressiveness, and there are times when it's not a stretch to ponder that they could easily jump from egg/scrap eaters to human flesh eaters. On a recent 3:30 a.m. walk to Ivania's house, in fact, Miriam almost experienced this dietary shift first hand as she was all but eaten by literally every dog that lives along the dusty road between our homes. Few of them, and certainly not Cujo the giant, black, ferocious killer dog, were at all dissuaded by her shouts and swings with the long, hard broom handle she was carrying. As a consequence, Miriam will not be making any more morning walks to Ivania's to cook enchiladas, as clearly walking softly and carrying a big stick only worked for Teddy Roosevelt.

Before we left Boston, we partnered with the boys' school (big props to Tucker Elementary!) to do a computer drive for Earth Day. The drive resulted in some fifteen donated computers and smartphones, and earlier this week two were given to the top performing students at Lechecuagos Secondary School. It's hard for us to truly appreciate the value of a second-hand computer, but to an aspiring student here with very little money, it is a game changer. Each computer came updated with lots of software, including Rosetta Stone

(English), and the two recipients were over the moon. Cully was asked to give a short speech in front of the four hundred student auditorium, and let's just say he's got some more Spanish studying to do. But, it was edifying to see one of our favorite expressions (Small Investment = Big Impact) play itself out once again here in Nicaragua.

One of the flagship programs for Tololamos is the *Vivero* (tree nursery) Project. Its first year was 2013, when they planted some 10,000 tree saplings and donated more than 8,000 to any community members who wanted to grow trees. This year, the project is ramping up again and we have been fortunate to be a part of it. We helped fill some of the more than 6,000 planting bags with soil, then last week we helped plant seeds in the bags. The planting part is a lot less labor intensive than the filling part, and it has been an education in horticulture for all of us.

The first day, we helped plant some 8 different species of trees, including ones with cool names like *acacia amarilla, madero negro, cortez negro, and laurel macho.* We subsequently helped plant four additional types of seeds, including *naranja, tamarindo* and both red and yellow *marañon*, the seeds of which Miriam and Adilsa gathered together from trees near our house earlier this week. The project is a great example of a Public-Private Partnership, as the seeds and bags are donated by the Ministry of Forestry, while the funds and the labor are provided by Tololamos. The cool thing is, more trees means less dust, healthier soil, cleaner lungs, less chronic health problems and ultimately a more productive local ecosystem. If all goes well, the saplings should be ready by the end of May. Come swing by and get one if you can.

Up until early this year, there was a sizeable market near the cathedral (the largest in Central America) in León. The market filled a whole street and stretched from the cathedral (the Spaniards ensured there was a church every couple blocks) almost all the way to Calvary Church, a few blocks east. Then one day, as with the post office, it just disappeared. Poof. It was a bit perplexing, because there were hundreds of vendors there, serving everything from shoes, to jewelry, to all sorts of *comida tipica* (local food). Actually, a part of the market remained as the tens of small *ferreteria* (hardware) stores that lined one side of the street were still there. Naturally, we were curious what had happened (this was how hundreds of people made their livelihood every day, for goodness sakes). After a bit of searching, we found our answer.

A whole new indoor market had been built in a massive space next to the old market (not readily visible from the street) and there you could find familiar faces and smells, all watched over by a Mary and a Jesus statue, each supervising the daily transactions from on high. One more thing about marketplaces; why is it that stores selling the same stuff (shoes, bikes, clothes, hardware) all congregate in one place? Kind of like the Burger King/McDonalds/Wendy phenomenon, stores serving basically the same merchandise (at least Mickey D's and BK have the Big Mac and Whopper to differentiate themselves, and Wendy's has chili) sit next to each other all throughout León, seemingly relying on luck and the caprices of their clients to shop with them instead of their next door neighbor. An economist would say it's because of economies of scale and concentration, but we're not so sure…

Lessons we've learned:

1. They say you're not supposed to stick cotton swabs in your ear, but come on, we all do it, right? The thing is, usually, if you're successful, they come out yellow. In El

Tololar, the yellow is generally coated in volcanic dust, so utilizing a second, or third Q-tip, is good practice.

2. Always shake out your shoes before putting on, both because it will keep your freshly laundered socks a little cleaner, and it can prevent scorpion bites.

3. Sweeping is useless. The floor will just get dirty again, so why sweep at all?

4. Sleeping (or trying to) is also useless at times. Inevitably, at that precise moment between wakefulness and slumber, Murphy will make sure that either a rooster will crow, a dog will bark, an errant bug will hit your mosquito net, or, infrequently, an earthquake will shake you awake. It's a given. Sleeping pills do help, but only a little.

5. Still trying to figure out what is harder, the rainy or dry season. If you were a mathematician, would this equate: gnats + ants + flies + sweeping water at midnight + moldy rooms and clothes + pig-infested puddles + power outages = crazy heat + no water + constant sweat + more scorpions + wind-driven dust + allergies.

Chapter 17:
Dream a Little Dream, Super-Human Kids, Dirty Like You Read About

Early April

Not long after we first arrived, we all had a chance to ride Don Leonel's horse on various occasions. He would proudly put a saddle on the small white *caballo* (name for male horses, *yegua* for females) and gently help hoist one of us up. We would ride in circles, or figure-eights, around his yard, slaloming in and around various coconut, grapefruit and peach trees. A few months later, Miriam and others helped nurse the same horse back to health after he was bitten on the neck by a vampire bat. Since then, the horse has largely remained idle most days, tied to a tree in the corner of Don Leonel's yard with a rope around his neck that always seems just a bit too tight for our liking. His main period of utility comes during the planting season in August and September, when he is connected to a plow to cultivate and prepare the soil for maize.

One of the problems with stallions here is that if you don't watch them like a hawk, they can go *vagando* – wandering – looking for other equally aimless females. The best way to minimize this wanderlust is castration, a procedure that immediately lessens their lecherousness, but horse castration here can be akin to civil war era medicine, where both the tool and it's bearer at times lack the education and cleanliness to ensure the job is accomplished in good order. Such may have been the case with this horse (as usual in Nicaragua it is exceedingly difficult to actually ascertain the name of any animals so we will call him just "horse"). We only learned of the operation when we saw horse's legs covered in blood one morning. We found out that he indeed had been castrated the day before, and indications were that he was healing quickly.

Things took a turn for the worse a few days later when horse stopped eating, and one day, while Miriam was helping Adilsa categorize books at the elementary library, Adilsa informed her that horse had died the night before. Aquiles and Chepe had been commissioned to dig the grave – not an easy job in sunbaked volcanic soil – and just like that he was gone. All that remained was his tree, rope, some stray poop that hadn't been raked, and various mounds of leftover food. He left so quietly, it was almost like he had never been there. But that's life here, and people don't get too attached to anything. They enjoy things when they are present, yet are ready to let them go when their time is up. It's not a bad philosophy.

There are these little fluffy, white pod-like things that have been floating around El Tololar recently. Some type of seed, now and again they come drifting past you. If you are lucky, one might even land on you. Olle has dubbed them "dreams," which is actually a pretty great name if you think about it, and maybe these white floaters are not so different from our own dreams. They often come flying in and out of our lives, something we think about from time to time but often neglect because they are hard to grasp. They can be ethereal, difficult to quantify, and even if we could catch them, we just don't know how to plant and water the seed that grows inside them. But what if we made the extra effort to snatch them up out of the air, letting that cottony, soft, smooth idea tarry in our hand, growing from a seed and gaining form and definition every day, turning from just a fleeting ambition into a concrete, achievable, actionable concern. What if…

Just before Christmas, we watched as Carmelo the pig gave birth to five piglets. Last Monday night, we ate her. We actually consumed her on several occasions, first in the form of *adobado* (a delicious pork dish prepared slightly differently depending on the Central American country you happen to be in. Nicaragua makes the delicacy with yucca, onions, garlic, peppers, and orange and lemon juice) then as fresh *chicharron* (pork rind) and finally *asado* (grilled) on a makeshift spit/barbecue we built in our backyard out of bricks left over from the construction of our house.

Carlos and Miriam had hoped we could be present at slaughter time, but fortunately (we were relieved we already had plans) we needed to go to León that day. Nonetheless, upon returning we received a blow by blow recap of the way it all went down, Carmelo first receiving a knock on the head with the butt end of an axe, followed by a knife to the throat. From there they hung her up to bleed her out, skinned her, and sold her off piecemeal (head and feet included) to an assortment of neighbors, most of whom had been previously warned that some serious ham was coming down the pipeline in short order.

It's weird to be talking about animals like this, especially ones you knew and saw on a daily basis every time you went to the latrine, but that is life here. Pigs are not pets, but a vital way for a family to make money, and Carmelo provided much needed funds in her passing. Still, it was a bit tough to engage in a conversation with neighbors when six giant strips of pork skin were hanging in the background, smiling at us, drying in the sun. Likewise, it was awkward when our neighbor Miriam came by with the freshly prepared *adobado*. She came upon

Cully in the kitchen in his boxers after having just bathed and our Miriam still in the shower, then weaving and dodging her scantily-clad way back to our room in the midst of Miriam and Carlos's elaborate pork presentation and hopeful anticipation of a positive appraisal by us. Perhaps it was Olle who said it best, that the *adobado* was second only to the Pizza Hut in León.

There is a magical place a few hours from our house called *Selva Negra.* The words mean "Black Forest" in Spanish, and the founders and owners of the giant nature reserve are from Germany, arriving in Nicaragua many years back with the intention of creating a biosphere akin to Germany's famous forest, albeit in a hotter climate with a whole different set of wildlife. We spent one afternoon there on the way back from our foiled Honduran border crossing attempt, and it almost felt like we were in a dream world. We sat by a lake sipping unbelievably delectable coffee that had been grown and roasted on the premises (Harlan and Olle sipped delectable cokes), had a scrumptious meal, and then embarked on a multi-hour hike into the woods.

Selva Negra has a variety of trails, and we chose one that passed an absolutely beguiling German-architecture inspired church in the middle of the quiet forest. From there we continued on, deep into the old-growth forest, listening to a panoply of bird calls and animal noises. We chose the trail that promised at least the possibility of both monkey and Quetzal sightings. We missed the monkeys but were tracking a pair of Quetzals, beautiful red, green, white and blue birds with insanely long tails that are almost a thing of legend due to their elusiveness. We hunted them for close to an hour, every so often hearing their unique shrill, in the process being led onto secondary and tertiary trails deeper into the massive forest. In the end we were granted only one brief glimpse, a colorfully adorned Quetzal swooshing overhead then quickly disappearing. But, our circuitous route provided one bonus experience we'll likely never forget.

Walking together on the soft, earthy trail, we stopped to listen for monkeys. All of a sudden, we heard a rustle in the leaves ahead of us. We froze, and watched as no less than thirty White-nosed Coatis (*Pizotes* in Spanish) crossed the trail directly in front of us. *Pizotes* look kind of like a raccoon, but with longer snouts and tails, and we were literally transfixed as the family (or herd, pod, gaggle, whatever word you use for a group of Coatis) crossed the trail, one after another, not even seeing us as we stood there like statues. The final *Pizote* that crossed was almost white in color (most are grayish-brown) and when the crossing was over, we just stood there, grinning with glee. We felt that kind of happiness you get only when you've witnessed something downright awe-inspiring in nature, some deep connection with the wild part of our souls that our house-bound, city-living, connected to metal and concrete bodies don't feel very often.

We've got a problem with scorpions. We're not sure if it is the location of our house, situated at ground zero for regular scorpion rendezvous or possibly the palm-thatched roof to our patio, providing a dry, dark place for alacránes (the local name for the ubiquitous Bark Scorpion). Whatever the reason, we've got a problem. In the rainy season (up until November) we saw them less, maybe once every two weeks. Now, and really in the last few weeks, the count has skyrocketed. It is not uncommon to have multiple sightings in a day, and what's all the more baffling is that our neighbors seem to be very surprised that we have seen so many.

Our problem got real on a recent Sunday morning when Olle, who normally wakes up first, started crying as he was trying to put on his clothes. We rushed over to unlock his door, which we have to lock most nights from the outside because of the powerful, door-blowing wind. He had definitely been bit or stung by something, a red mark evident on his chest, but we couldn't find anything. Only a few minutes later when Miriam was engaged in a second, more vociferous clothe-shaking session did we see it, a tiny guy (fortunately), about the width of a nickel, happily curled up on the sleeve of Olle's shirt. We killed him with gusto and due to Olle's toughness and the scorpion's diminutive size, we made out with just a few tears.

Harlan, too, dodged a scorpion-bullet the following day. He had just arrived at school and was looking for a pencil in the zipper pocket of his backpack. Thankfully, he looked before he grabbed, as a sizable scorpion crawled out, clearly confused as to how he had arrived at Rebekah Rivas Elementary School. The scorpion definitely rued the day, as really the last place you want your maiden backpack voyage to end is in the midst of a gaggle of Nicaraguan sixth-grade boys, several of whom were more than happy to assist Harlan in terminating Scorpio right then and there.

We thought the skinny, brownish, speckled dog who lives at Adilsa's, one we've dubbed both Fuera and Humpy on different occasions, actually was her pet. It turns out, he is in reality our neighbor Miriam's dog, although even she doesn't seem to be aware of this. Even more disconcerting then Humpy's obvious lack of domicile is the fact that recently he's gotten a case of the bite-sies. First he bit Esteban's niece, then Beto was nipped on the leg while riding his moto. Most recently Beto's son Michael, playing one Saturday morning with Olle and Rachel was bit by Humpy, right on the *pompis* (butt). Michael, only four-years old, became both the first butt-bite victim and another patient of Miriam's, who doctored his behind with loving kindness, hydrogen peroxide and some Band-Aids. Biting dogs can be a problem, though, and while Michael's rear has healed up nicely, Humpy, aka Fuera, will need to be dealt with in the strictest of ways if he keeps this up.

"It's kind of incredible, we still have water at 9 a.m.," remarked Miriam one recent Sunday morning. Water has been particularly sparse around El Tololar over the past two months, and we generally have water from when we wake up at 5:15 until about 8 a.m. or so, when the taps run dry. Weekends seem to be even worse, with Sunday usually being the driest day of all. We've learned to manage the water scarcity, but recently the big tank that serves most of El Tololar broke. Generally when that happens, it can be at least four days without water. In fact, as of this writing we are on day seven without water and no *agua* in sight. We are fortunate living as we do on the Rivas compound, as they have an electric, well-fed tank of their own that almost always has water (electricity outages notwithstanding). Thus, in a pinch, we can usually shower, get extra water for washing dishes or clothes, or even procure water for the garden.

Most people are not that lucky and when the big tank goes on the fritz, they have to travel back in time. They saddle their horse or yolk their ox, tie a long rope to a relatively small bucket, and hoist pail after pail of water up to the surface, often from depths of up to eighty meters. You do that a few times, and you really begin to appreciate water. A few family's wells have dried up long ago, and they have to rely on the kindness of strangers for water. The Rivas family is incredibly generous and over the course of last weekend, various bottle-toting neighbors stopped by to fill up.

Going without water has lots of secondary effects that go beyond not being able to shower, wash your clothes, or that other important thing… oh yeah, drink. We witnessed this first hand in connection with the *Vivero* (Tree Nursery) Project. April is the hottest month in El Tololar, and most days it breaks 100 degrees, easy. Nascent trees need lots of TLC, and at least double daily dosages of water. The recent water outage meant Denis, the man responsible for taking care of the seedlings, was in a bit of a pickle as his *pozo* (well) was also dry. His only option was to use nearby *pozo* and bring buckets of water by horse cart back to the plants, but he lacked a long enough rope to haul the water up eighty meters from the aquifer. We happened to be in León that day, and said we'd bring the rope to Denis in a taxi (Larry, the amazing soccer player's dad, Paolo, has a taxi and at times we call on him for a ride).

Like most voyages in Nicaragua, this one proved to be an adventure. We met Paolo a block east of La Union supermarket as the road was closed due to construction. He drove us past Beto's office where we picked up the eighty-two meters of rope from Wilmar, who had just procured it. Our goal was to get back as quick as possible so that Denis and his son Erickson could start hauling water but Paolo wanted to show us his house, his pig, and his other son. Having taken care of that errand, we headed straight to Tololar, that is until Paulo's first wife and our neighbor, Paula, called asking for a ride so that she and her co-worker, *La Doctora*, could attend a funeral.

Tragically, a young boy from El Tololar had been killed in a freak hunting accident the night before. We turned around, headed back to León, and waited for them at the bust stop. They finally arrived, and we managed to squeeze all eight of us into the little taxi, Familia Lundgren plus our friend Leo in the back, Paulo at the helm, and Paula and La Doctora mooshed in the front, alternating mutual cheek placement for maximum comfort. Despite our delayed arrival, we handed the rope off to Denis, hoping it was in time for him to make several thousand seedlings very happy that afternoon.

Cully had the chance to visit a fascinating gentleman named Mario at his small *finca* (farm) last week. Mario was one of the trailblazers who helped make Cerro Negro – the nearby active volcano that people surf – a real tourism project. In fact, according to Mario, it was his son who first attempted to 'surf' down the volcano. You can imagine how early conversations about the prospect of surfing may have gone: "Hey, check out that hot, gnarly-looking, active volcano over there! Yes, the one over there that could erupt any minute. I was thinking, what if we grab some wood planks, throw some aluminum on the bottom for strength and better glide, and launch over the wicked-steep side? Really, what could go wrong?" But Mario is about much more than surfing volcanoes, and his own personal history includes a stint fighting with the Sandinistas some forty years back under the pseudonym *La Puma*. Now his farm boasts perhaps a greater variety of animals than any other *finca* in Nicaragua. In fact, in Cully's short time there, he encountered the following types of fauna:

- one giant parrot who almost bit his finger off
- two medium parrots who tried to speak, unsuccessfully
- three small parakeets, one strangely bald

- one deer who looked like he needed a friend
- one huge owl who wouldn't stop looking at Cully no matter where he went, clearly ready to tear his head off
- ten rabbits, five dogs, several iguanas
- two geese, the male whom feigned attacks on Cully on at least four occasions
- ducks, chickens, turkeys, and lots of their babies
- And a partridge, this one choosing a mango over a pear tree.

Mario is not only an animal lover but also a visionary. In addition to him and his wife's efforts to make Cerro Negro one of the premier tourist destinations in Nicaragua, he is in the process of building a huge pool on his property. It really is an ingenious business idea – the only other public pool we know of is ten miles away in Telica – that has potential, especially once we get water back! Perhaps what struck Cully most about Mario was his deep love of humanity. Near the end of their conversation, Mario, talking about why he is on this earth, said, "We are not here to do things alone. We are here on earth to address physical, emotional, spiritual and economic needs of our families and our community. Our community is big, it is really the whole earth. And we are all brothers and sisters, no matter what our color or religion." Maybe we can all learn a thing or two from Mario.

As we approached one year without having our teeth cleaned, we decided it was finally time to go see the dentist. First, we made a series of appointments for the whole family, one right after another. We arrived on time and in general the cleanings went well. They took twice as long as the *dentista* had said they would, but the experience – and quality of care – was even better than expected. We were especially excited that she used the little sucky contraption that suctions up all your drool, saving us from having to rinse and spit every five minutes. However, closer examination of both adult's teeth revealed two cavities for Cully, and the need for a new crown for Miriam.

One week later we were back at her office for round two. The procedure on Cully's mouth was largely successful, even though one filling took a solid 1 and a half hours to complete (what the heck was she doing in there?). The only negative outcome was that some of the leftover cavity filling material remained in between a few teeth, making flossing virtually impossible in some locations. Miriam's routine went well enough, except that for some reason she was not permitted to move her jaw or body for close to two hours, resulting in a quasi-lockjaw situation and cramping in her lower extremities, both which cleared up quickly. The larger issue was that the cap procedure she had gone in for, necessary due to a prior root canal, was never was performed. Instead, the dentist chose to fill the tooth as if it were a cavity. Hopefully, it will all come out in the wash…

It wasn't supposed to be that arduous, but with the thermometer pushing 103 degrees, every step began to feel like it was through concrete. Actually, our steps were only through dust, but a lot of it and with every pace, a mini dust bomb of talcum-like powder would go off around your feet, rising quickly as it stuck to you or your hiking buddy's legs, arms, neck and lungs. We had caught the 7 a.m. bus out of El Tololar, heading to the town of San Jancinto for an overnight hike. There, our friend and *guia* (guide) Yader had planned for us to begin our ascent of Volcano Telica. If you ever want a

Nicaraguan hiking guide, we can highly recommend Yader, who was so conscientious that he engaged in not one but two separate reconnaissance missions prior to our hike, just to make sure all would go smoothly, which it did… mostly.

Including Yader's brother Fernando, a budding artist and also possibly a future *guia*, our group of six left the hot-spring tourist town of San Jancinto and headed up, first through fallow, dusty fields of corn and beans. Along the way – when we could see through the clouds of dust – Yader introduced us to a variety of Nicaraguan wildlife. We learned that the national bird, the *guardarbarranco* (translated "the guarder of banks") always builds its nests in dirt overhangs and banks such as those we were passing, a sly move except for when its main prey, big snakes, enters and eats it. We passed the nests of *correcoyote* wasps, hanging conspicuously in nearby trees and according to Yader, not dangerous unless provoked, and then very dangerous!

We had multiple glimpses of the relatively rare *Alma de Perro* (Soul of the Dog) bird, as well as parrots, beautifully adorned orioles, and a bizarre, road-runner looking bird that even Yader had never seen. We stopped for lunch under a giant mango tree, and witnessed Yader and Fernando do their best Laurel and Hardy impersonation as they simultaneously tried to set up a hammock (unsuccessfully), hit iguanas with slingshot, and dodge a giant hill of ants that had begun to dive into the pork their mother Myra had freshly grilled that morning. The hilarious set of events finally ended with Fernando tripping over the pork, and Miriam laughing uncontrollably.

The hike wasn't all laughs though, and after two extended stops to beat the heat and water breaks every five minutes, we arrived at a huge field, situated on a giant, grassy plain rimmed with palm trees, just below Telica's massive crater. We gathered wood for the night's fire, and then headed straight up to the crater, and huge billows of sulfuric gas. The Lundgren family all began to cough as we approached the crater, but it didn't seem like a huge deal at first. Miriam and Olle, though, felt the worst of it and they decided it was best to head down. As they descended, Miriam's lungs tightened up even more and it was clear that without help, things were going to get a bit dicey. It was then that Super Olle arrived, leaving Miriam and sprinting at full tilt across the volcanic field, retrieving her inhaler at light speed and returning in time to save the day. Olle, you are a superhero!

The rest of our trip up Telica was less eventful, except for a few singular experiences. First, we encountered a giant, animal, sniffing and grunting outside our three-person tent for half the night. The giant creature, which made our hair, even what is left of Cully's, stand on end, was later found to be a resident, semi-wild horse. We also had the out-of-body experience of crawling on hands and knees to the actual edge of the crater. We took turns holding Yader's hand while we each peered over the precipice into the red lava fire, and listened to the roaring power of the belly of the earth. As the raw, raging force simmered below us, we felt a preternatural sense of awe. Somehow, laying with our hands clasped together on the moon-like surface, we sensed we could collectively achieve anything, and that all the in-fighting and real polarization that was happening back home could be resolved. If only everyone had a personal volcano to commune with once in a while. During that experience, Harlan made the astute comment that, "I hate it when it gets windy when we are near a crater on an active volcano," and of course he was right.

Upon arriving back home the following day, we all agreed that the hike had been an incomparable success. We also concluded that because of the combination of heat, sweat, and dust, we likely were dirtier than we had ever been in our lives, and that is not easy to do!

Chapter 18:
Killer Bees, Boys in Black, That was Shocking!

Mid-April

International Development is really about working collaboratively to determine and deploy resources to solve problems and improve lives. The development organization we are partnering with here in El Tololar – Tololamos – is small, especially compared to some of the giant US-based organizations that exist. But they are also really smart, for three reasons:

1. They listen to the people around them – the beneficiaries of their projects.
2. They always incorporate lessons learned into future programs.
3. They adapt to a constantly changing world.

Take the case of the water pumps they have installed in several locations around El Tololar over the past few years. Along with local Tololamos representatives Wilmar and Beto, Familia Lundgren had the opportunity to visit two of the homes where pumps (and water irrigation capabilities) have been installed. Quite a vetting process went into identifying the candidates (depth of well, total area to be irrigated, types of crops, access to sufficient electricity sources, distance from transportation, potential of system to increase economic situation of family, etc.) and both families we visited started out as stellar candidates.

The first family had quite a lot of land (5 *manzanas* – equal to about 12 acres). We arrived on motorcycles – three on each – and were ushered into their backyard (basically across the street from Rebekah Rivas Elementary School where Harlan and Olle attend) by a guy with a stick meant to keep away their reportedly ferocious dogs. They never materialized, and we came upon the owner brushing his teeth, surrounded by about 200 bees and wasps, none of which were given a second look by the locals. He had lifted the pump out of the sixty-meter well and while he fetched the heavy contraption (it looks kind of like a mini, meter-long, silver torpedo) Beto began testing the electrical connections. He then hooked up the pump, set it in a nearby deep water basin, and hit the power switch on the electrical box. A bird had made a sizable nest on top of the box and even though we were hungry, we weren't prepared for fried bird that early and were relieved when the electricity buzzed to life with no shocks or zaps. The pump worked perfectly, humming and pumping water just as advertised. So what was the problem?

Further conversation with the family – interrupted three times by four, ornery geese looking to stake out their territory – revealed that the current dry season had been especially severe (we can definitely attest to this) and the water-level in their well had dropped so low that the pump, even when sitting on the bottom, just couldn't find enough water to pump. So it would either shut off, or start to fry itself trying to pump thin air. But there is more to the narrative than that, as we soon came to find out.

All across El Tololar, water levels have been slowly dropping in the underground aquifers, a process that has sped up with changes to the local climate; longer dry seasons followed by ever shorter and less reliable wet seasons. The low water levels, however, have been exacerbated by other, semi-sinister actors who have come onto the scene as of late. Two very wealthy families have bought up huge tracts of land in El Tololar. Subsequently, they have installed state-of-the-art, extremely expensive water systems and begun planting various crops, including sugarcane, crops that can have very high water requirements. They have paid for the water (at subsidized rates it's not much for them) and received the blessing of the local water committee, a few of whom likely made a nice bonus on the deal. Actually, according to some of our neighbors, it is more than 'likely' that the water officials are making a pretty penny from their job. In fact, ever since a potable water system was installed in El Tololar, some 15 years back, the same 3-5 people have been on the committee, and financially, they are all doing very, very well.

In life, everything is interrelated and it is rare that any one thing is the sole cause of anything, but it's hard not to see the clear impact that money and power – and corruption – are having here in El Tololar. The wealthy, out-of-towners get their water, and the locals watch their wells run dry; corrupt local officials make decisions that benefit themselves at the expense of the community. Of course there are many layers to this story, and one is that we in the 'developed' world use water to our hearts content – playing our own role in depleting global water sources. Let's face it, our droughts (except perhaps Californians) haven't yet reached the point where we can't take a bath, wash our clothes, or have a fresh glass of water.

But the times they are a changin, everywhere, and the day will come when the whole underground aquifer here in El Tololar will dry up. Or, perhaps closer to home, that inhabitants of *Anytown*, USA, will have much larger sacrifices to make than skipping a few days of watering their lawn. A solution? Use less water, and plant more trees. How can we help? For starters, initiate a 'bucket' day at your own home. Fill up several buckets of water one morning (2-4 gallons a person), and that is all your family gets that day for washing clothes, cooking, showering, brushing teeth, drinking, etc. Try it, it's fun, and a great lesson.

The water pump (*bomba*) at the second house actually worked fine as well. The reason they wanted the pump removed is in some ways for much more practical reasons. The owner of the home runs a motorcycle-repair shop in his front yard. His business keeps him busy enough and he just doesn't have the time to make use of the system to irrigate his land; plus the fact that one of his wells is also dry.

So Tololamos is addressing these two problems head on, speaking with the owners, listening to their challenges. They are coming up with solutions that make sense, possibly redeploying the pumps in other locations with deeper wells, or with people who have more time to allocate. They are fixing, repairing, spreading and digging for answers and solutions that can only be found with hard work, common sense, sweat equity, and local ingenuity.

It was always kind of a *when* and *where*, not an *if* question. "When would Miriam get stung by a scorpion?" Turns out it was on a typical Tuesday night, about 6:20 p.m., as she was in the middle of cooking a delicious pasta dinner. She had reached for our dish drying towel – one she had already used that very evening several times to no ill effect – when

WHAM, a not insignificant scorpion's tail stroked her right index finger. Adilsa was just coming over to see if we wanted to play the locally popular card game of casino, and she, Cully and Miriam congregated in the kitchen around the cursed towel. A flip of a fold revealed the aggressor, and it only took a few wallops to put it down – permanently. First Miriam's finger and then her hand puffed up massively, and within 30 minutes *thee wath thalking thort of thunny*, because her tongue too had begun to swell, a calling card of sorts that scorpions often leave with their victims. The pain was pretty bad, and somehow she managed to pick up and drink her wine successfully while dealing, and ultimately winning the game of casino. She was better the next morning but 24 hours after the strike she still had a swollen finger; bad Scorpion!

About a week after our cat *Dulce* died, we acquired another one, thanks to the generosity of Johanna, supposedly one of Adilsa's cousins – really, is everyone in this community related? Cully had met Johanna one morning at the boy's school and they had struck up a conversation about cats as Cully ate one of Johanna's freshly made enchiladas. It turns out that Johanna had an extra feline lying around, and if he stopped by that afternoon, he could have it. Cully brought with him the resident animal expert Olle, who gave a thumbs up when Johanna's daughter brought out the gray and white cat that, ironically, already possessed one of Miriam's nicknames – Mimi.

Olle carried Mimi home with Cully across several peanut fields, in a bag and during a rather ferocious windstorm, and she has been with us ever since – except perhaps for the very first night when she scaled our concrete wall at midnight in order to get out of our room. Mimi soon started to get plumper, and most bets were that she would have three babies. After Olle had already divined that her suddenly heavy breathing must signify something, she did in fact give birth to three kittens underneath our bed, our whole family having the rather rare opportunity (even 78-year-old Don Leonel has never seen a cat in labor) to see the births unfold in all their raw, beautiful, grouse glory.

Sometimes it's the mundane that can really annoy – like getting dirt on your wet feet while putting your sandals on post-shower; or having bugs in your coffee because you forgot to turn your mug upside down the night before. Removing chicken poop from your shoes is bothersome, as is getting the dirt off the bottom of the pee bucket you are trying to clean and bleach. It's no fun when no matter how hard you scrub, you complete your bucket shower only marginally less etched in dirt than when you started or when your freshly-washed clothes are sitting on an ant hill and not the line, because a huge gust of wind blew them away. Getting your pants stuck on a barbed-wire fence happens almost daily (although our fence-crossing skills have improved heaps since we arrived) and it can be just plain uncomfortable when you have to peel your leg skin off of the 100 degree vinyl school bus seat. Getting semi-electrocuted is kind of a drag as well.

Our electricity system, like many here, has been, for lack of a better word, Jerry-rigged (thanks, Jerry). We have tapped into Miriam and Carlos's water and electric systems, both having been extended to our house from theirs. It seems to be a common practice here, and the system-sharing approach has worked smoothly, with us paying them approximately half the bill every month. Our outlets usually work pretty well, but for two issues.

First, most of our plugs just won't stay in the outlet to charge something. Our remedy is usually finding a small *chunche* – (a 'thing, in the local vernacular) like a book of matches, a tube of chapstick, or a bottle top. By squeezing the items between two plugs, the pressure is usually sufficient to hold both in place. Second, the electric current emanating from the outlets is a bit unpredictable, and we all have been 'zapped' several times. In fact, it's become commonplace enough that last week when Harlan yelled from his room in pain, our response went like this: "Was that a scorpion?" "No, I think he just got electrocuted." "Oh, okay, cool."

We had heard stories of men and boys, ghost-like apparitions, coated in thick black oil, terrorizing innocent bystanders, families and entire villages across Nicaragua during *Semana Santa* (Holy Week). But the stories were so far-fetched, it was hard to believe they were actually true. As the time drew near, we waited for them, not knowing whether to hide or face them. We locked up our valuables, and even moved our soap inside from our outdoor shower, as we heard that soap was a sought after, post-ritual cleaning product. Thursday came and went with no sign of them.

On Good Friday, in the company of 75 other pilgrims, we began to see the black figures, lining the dusty main road into El Tololar. We were part of the *Via Crucis* procession, walking from the preschool teacher's house (on this day the heavy structure with Jesus on top was stationed at her home) to the church, located downtown. We started with a short prayer, and began to walk, stopping at every house that had put a cross and flags – many of them ornately designed – outside their house, representing one of the stops Jesus made on his way to his crucifixion site. Each house with a cross, it seemed, was also required by tradition to give every pilgrim a plastic bag of *fresco* (local, ice-cold drinks that come in a wide variety of flavors and colors including chia, pineapple, cacao, banana, orange, tamarind, and melon). By the time we had reached the third cross, Cully had taken over Jesus-carrying duties – along with three, strapping young chaps from the village – and Miriam and the boys were following behind, singing, needing to use the toilet, and carrying an ever-increasing load of icy but quickly warming drinks.

The cross (metal and filled with concrete) was heavy, and new porters would step in from time to time to relieve weary bearers. The temperature was also heating up rapidly, and soon shade became pretty hard to come by. Apparently one woman – who we later found out broke her leg the following day while swimming at the ocean – felt the procession was actually moving too quickly. In order to decelerate, she took to walking at a snail's pace, directly in front of Cully and the other front hauler. She neglected to inform the people in the rear of the abrupt slowdown, and it was all Cully could do to stop from tripping over her and upsetting the whole Jesus cart, by this time adorned with lots of bouquets of beautiful flowers.

By the time we reached the church, everyone was sweating profusely, and most people were carrying 3-4 extra *frescos*, finding it humanly impossible to ingest the approximately ten drinks allotted to each marcher. There, also, we encountered the greatest number of men and boys in black. The origins of the tradition are a bit hazy, but the result is that up to thirty males, ranging in age from 17-40 (some people just can't stop) smear their bodies in thick, black oil. They fabricate elaborate headdresses out of old boxes, or put on masks – Darth Vader made an appearance, as did a pregnant King Kong – and march with sharp sticks, following the *Via Crucis* but also terrorizing young children at their homes.

The combination of hot sun, copious chemicals on skin, dehydration and likely alcohol consumption can and has resulted – this may come as a shock – in multiple hospital visits over the years. Somehow though, the whole experience, (opposing forces, heat, exhaustion, the weight of the cross) as manufactured as it may have been, imparted to us and our fellow walkers a better understanding of what Jesus' experience was like, many moons ago.

Sometimes, it feels good to be anonymous; to go about our business in our own private bubbles; to stay apart from others. It can feel like we have more control of what we do, when we can just be alone with our family in our house, or drive inconspicuously to the store at night, buying what we want, the cashier really the only other person who knows what we're doing. It's not like that for *Familia* Lundgren in El Tololar. Being the resident gringos, everyone both knows who we are and what we do. They know when we are going to León, because they see us take the bus. They know when we've been shopping, and how much we've bought, because we come home with big bags of stuff. They know when we leave our home, because they see us walking as a family down the dusty streets. Sometimes, it can be aggravating to lose your anonymity. But, in the end, it is part of being in community. When we know each other, we can help one another. We can be support systems because we understand what our neighbor is going through, and some of the challenges they face. We can go from being self-centered to other-centered. That's where the goodness is found.

Nicaraguans are geniuses at finding ways to extend the lives of things. Take hammocks, for example. Since we arrived, we have always had two hammocks hanging underneath our patio. They – like our shopping bags and

Harlan and Olle's beds – are made of this stringy, nylon material that is actually incredible strong. The boy's *tijera* (scissor*)* beds are still going strong 8 months in, and while the colorful bags we use to do our shopping are frayed, they still work for hauling groceries from León twice a week. The hammock that hangs in front of Miriam's verdant garden (currently sporting tomatoes, swiss chard, and a second round of succulent, volunteer watermelon) finally bit the dust last week, a gaping hole opening up first near where a person's butt is positioned and finally along the length of the hammock.

But there is always more use in things – like the second-hand clothes so many friends and family have donated – and our hammock has gone on to live second lives as a punching bag, basketball hoop, watermelon-holder and sled. The next time something breaks, rips or spontaneously combusts in your house, try your hand at being a true Nicaraguan (many of you surely already are) and fixing it. You'll be helping the environment and enhancing your problem-solving skills. Buy new only as a last option, an option that a lot of people here don't even have.

Harlan has a goal; to juggle a soccer ball with his feet one hundred times before we leave. He's been practicing with Cully, most late afternoons when the hottest of the hot is over, underneath Don Leonel's grapefruit tree. He hasn't got there yet, but the goal is in sight. Setting goals is great no matter what your age, and Harlan is learning to keep his eyes on the prize.

Mangoes are starting to hit tables pretty hot and heavy and with at least seven types to choose from, it's hard to go wrong. They are all delicious, the only variety we haven't liked thus far is *Mango Liso*, an exceptionally stringy version that requires access to floss almost immediately after eating. Although delicious, mangoes also can cause skin allergies and Cully spent a good one and a half weeks scratching a deep red, poison ivy like, mango-induced rash. Miriam and Olle also recently had allergies. We think their allergies were heat-induced, as 100 degree plus heat, combined with sweat and dust, can wreak havoc on your skin.

We continue to hold our movie nights, once every three weeks or so. Last Sunday was the first ever premier in El Tololar of the movie *Secretariat.* Everyone in El Tololar either has a horse or knows one, and word must have got out, as we had our biggest showing yet (twenty-six people). Olle had already seen the movie a few times, and wasn't a big fan of all the boring stuff that happened in between the races. So he decided, what the heck, I'll try and build a circuit in the kitchen. Grabbing batteries, a light bulb, electrical wire and a knife, he had at it on the concrete kitchen floor, cutting, connecting and taping in between quick Derby, Preakness and Belmont peeks. Ultimately, his circuit didn't work, but he gave it a shot. Often, that's the most important part, the process, not the result.

When we were kids, we heard seemingly outlandish stories about Africanized killer bees invading the USA from Mexico, perhaps much like the current administration views immigrants. In actuality, these bees are for real, and we recently witnessed them on multiple occasions. First, Don Leonel informed us as we were returning from a run in the peanut field that we should avoid walking by Paula's house (two down from ours) because some of the bees had set up shop in her son Larry's bedroom. Perhaps they chose wisely, as Larry (the world-class soccer player) is literally the quickest person we've ever met and thus the only individual who could outrun them in a pinch.

Ignoring Don Leonel's advice, we walked over to Paula's with Miriam and Carlos and from a safe distance, observed some hundreds of bees swarming in and around Larry's room. Our short conversation resulted in us collectively considering a variety of assault plans on the bees, with options including starting a fire in Larry's room to smoke them out, building a fire just outside his door, fumigating the room with gasoline, or sterilizing it with a local insect killer called *ciperimetrina.* We left the conversation to make dinner, and later found out that hard-core, 78-year-old Don Leonel had thrown caution to the wind himself and gone in with a tank of chemicals attached to his back. He disinfected the whole room and forced the hive to at least relocate, despite suffering himself from frequent allergies to bee stings. You don't mess with Don Leonel.

The next day, while we were preparing for home school, we heard a loud, humming noise, emanating at first from somewhere near Esteban's house. The buzzing decibel level increased as it went by our house – our imaginations going wild about what the killer bees might do to us – and then stopped at the corner of Carlos and Miriam's house. There, the killer bees set up shop, just outside an old tree stump. We watched from a distance as the droning noise slowly died down. When we looked again, they were gone. Our neighbors told us they tend to increase this time year, and we hope the approaching rainy season will end their swarming activities.

A smile so often begets a smile, doesn't it? Miriam has a great smile, and she's been sharing it around El Tololar. In spite of the challenges of living here – and there are many – she finds a way to share a big *senyum* (smile) everywhere she goes. And a smile is all the more important when you are trying to make contact with someone in a different language, and when you come from different cultures. When our family gets on the local bus, for example, people are often either confused as to why we are there, or perhaps too shy to strike up a conversation. But a big smile, followed by a polite, "*como estas*?" can go a long way in building relationships. And smiles work both ways; on many a hot, sweaty, dusty day, it has been a cheery smile from a stranger that has lifted our spirits and made us new.

Chapter 19:
Hare-Raising Tales, Painting By Numbers, One Bad-A___ Hombre

Late April/Early May

We love Don Leonel. He is a supremely unique, hard-working, caring, personality, the local Godfather, and at times possessing an accent eerily similar (albeit in Spanish) to Marlon Brando. Conversations with Don Leonel can and do happen almost anywhere around the Rivas compound, but his favorite place to relax is in his backyard, underneath several papaya trees, swinging slowly in his hammock while listening to the radio. On many occasions we have come upon him there, and quickly launched into discussions on any number of topics. A recent conversation, typical of most in length and breadth, hit on the following disparate yet somehow connected subjects: sharks, constellations, gangs, horses, motorcycles, dogs, cats, Donald Trump, the invention of flight, Daniel Ortega, the Silk Road, the Nile River, immigration and crocodiles. This *hombre* is a walking encyclopedia, adding new pages to his book every day.

But Don Leonel is more than a talker, and his wisdom has not been easily gained, instead slowly emerging as a result of a very difficult life; he definitely went to the school of hard knocks. He was one of nine siblings, all but he and his older brother Feliz have since passed away. He grew up in El Tololar, moving to different locations within the community as they suited his growing family (eight kids) at any given time.

He worked long hours, clearing fields of sugarcane and cotton with only his sweat and a machete, walking to the fields (now most workers take motorcycles) for 1 and a half hours each way, every day. His younger siblings slowly passed away over the years, succumbing to a usual set of infirmities and accidents that affect so many here; run over by a tractor, unintentionally shot with a gun, alcoholism, and kidney failure. He has contracted malaria more times than he can count, and has been witness to most of the trials and tribulations that have hit Nicaragua in the past half century or more; earthquakes (the 1972 quake killed at least 6,000), volcano eruptions, war. In the midst of it all, Don Leonel has persevered, raising a family of amazing individuals who themselves are fighting to endow Nicaraguans with more opportunities. Clearly, the fruit doesn't fall far from the tree.

Don Leonel is still going strong, as evidenced by the way he nonchalantly decided to break his mare a couple weeks back. Seated sideways and behind her on a cart, he navigated through multiple fence lines and across several corn fields, his body jostling as pieces of wood flew off the back. The horse was frightened, and to heighten the tension, her foal kept running in front of the cart, threatening to spill the entire load of wood, including Don Leonel. Somehow, he managed to steer her successfully to his house after his third wood-gathering trip. We can't be sure but think we heard him let out a couple *yee-haws* as he rounded the final corner.

As scary as Miriam's scorpion bite was, we recently heard that Aquiles also once got stung by a big scorpion. The injury produced the normal pain at the site, numb tongue, and in his case, dizziness and a headache. Strangely, the prick created an additional side effect that must have been downright alarming at the time but when told by a healthy Aquiles, came across as absolutely hilarious. For a brief period after the sting, Aquiles, despite his most strenuous efforts, evidently could only manage to walk backwards. His reverse ambulation and other side effects corrected themselves rather quickly, but stories of a retreating Aquiles are now part of Rivas family lore.

Normally when you order a hamburger, you get a hamburger – not necessarily in Nicaragua. Here once you've made your initial choice, you need to further specify if you want your *hamburguesa* made out of beef (a solid option), chicken, or pork. Are we missing something here?

As the previous hambur-graph was being written, Aquiles called us over to his house to see the *zorro* (possum) he had cornered in his tree. Different dictionaries we've consulted have alternately translated *zorro* as either skunk or fox, so finding a treed possum was a surprise. Aquiles, definitely a pacifist and someone who wouldn't willingly kill a flea (or tarantula as we found out previously) explained that the Nicaraguan version has a pretty basic diet; chickens, eggs, and possibly kittens. With our two chickens roosting yards away and our three baby kittens not much farther, we were ok with him doing what needed to be done, as long as we didn't have to watch.

It's kind of like clockwork – the rain starts and the electricity stops. It hasn't really started full force, but the evening of April 24th we experienced our first rain since November. It wasn't a deluge, but it produced enough liquid to wet the ground, leak water onto Olle's bed, and produce some beautiful lightning storms, which knocked out power for most of the night. Here, the clocks also work with respect to bugs; the rain starts and the bugs start biting.

Over the last week or so, we have definitely seen the fly, gnat and even mosquito populations increase, some of them graciously joining us for our morning exercises (aww, you shouldn't have, fellas), others landing on us during mealtimes. The most invasive bugs are the ones that come out at night, congregating around our two patio lights and in our kitchen, as if it was some sort of insect rave. Literally hundreds of little black bugs fly to the lights after even the slightest whisper of rain. They get fried and fall to the floor, where they make for crispy snacks for our two chickens. The other night time bug variety we call the kamikaze, a giant beetle with a faulty navigation system that somehow always manages to land in your drink, smack you in the head, or land in a plastic bag, where it produces a vibration so loud we often think we have a pet rattlesnake.

Miriam and Cully recently read an article in the *La Prensa* newspaper as we drove home on the 4:30 p.m. bus. The article's headline was that some seventy percent of Nicaraguans want to stay in their country, and not immigrate to other destinations, the two most popular being the USA and Costa Rica. The article went on to say that in fact almost 75% of those polled approve of Daniel Ortega, and think he is managing the country in the right direction. Unless you have been residing under a rock, if you are living in Nicaragua you know this is not accurate. It is interesting, though, that Ortega won this past November's elections with a similar ratio of victory. But really, it's not hard to achieve such great polling numbers when your family owns (or has close ties to) virtually every major, successful company in the country, including the entire Fourth Estate. What can we do to battle unchecked authority and duplicity in our own countries? At the very least, question authority and power, for where they reside, often so does their cousin, corruption. Ask the tough questions, and force those in control to be accountable for their actions.

We all love paint, don't we? It can transform the most lackluster wall or ceiling into a work of art. In the United States we generally don't think much about what paint actually costs but here in Nicaragua, it can actually be the single most important determining indicator of wealth. That's right, your blue, yellow or green house means you have more money than your neighbor. In El Tololar, it doesn't mean you are rich (no one is) but it means you have at least some disposable income. We live in a yellow house (at least on 3 sides) and so we are rich, not that this was ever a question. Adilsa painted half her bathroom with a three-times, watered down mixture of water and red paint, her lavatory sporting a dull, peach color that still brightens things up. So she has more than some of her neighbors, but not much more.

But the income/wealth/poverty scale doesn't end with colors. The next step down is the house made out of brick, but then covered with concrete, often a luxury for finishing walls. Farther down the local housing spectrum is the brick and mortar homes with tin roofs – there are many – followed by houses made from slabs of corrugated metal. The poorest of the poor live in shacks, cobbled together with metal, pieces of wood, and worn plastic tarps. Families in these houses definitely live on the edge. In fact, Aquiles' two beautiful daughters, Gabriela and Cindy, live in such a house with their mother, not far from the secondary school. A variety of events took place, some of them due to a corrupt legal system, which led to Cindy and Gabriel living in such abject conditions. And Cindy, the youngest, lives in fear. She has recurring nightmares. And why? Several years back, a drunk man in El Tololar entered a house by cutting through the thin plastic sheet that surrounded it. He kidnapped and then killed the child; and so Cindy is scared. She wishes instead she could live within the safe, concrete walls of her father Aquiles' house.

One of us, not mentioning any names, recently got sick, like really sick. The infirmity started innocently enough – we all pegged it on a fish taco. The first night the fish all came back up with a vengeance, but that wasn't the end of it. The next three days were spent fighting through a variety of daily activities (including hiking a volcano), the gut's ability to fend off waves of nausea strong enough to mitigate the worst effects, but never quite kicking the bug. Three nights after contraction (if in fact it was the fish taco) the flood gates opened late one night. The experience gave new meaning to the term "coming out both ends," and was exacerbated by the fact that our victim had to break a sacred rule; don't poo in the pee bucket. In fact lots of hygienic rules were breached that night and into the next day, including rule # 13: don't let the chickens and dogs in your garbage pit after dumping your full buckets of puke. But we made it through to live another day. Our three baby kittens, still sequestered under a bed with eyes closed, may have found the whole evening terrifying, however, wondering what in God's name the big wide world had in store for them when they finally left the safety of the cozy, under-bed area.

Cully took a walk to our friend Elio's house last week. Elio is the Cuban man who married a local woman from Tololar about 13 years ago, and has been here ever since. He is a very generous man, and because he lived in the states for many years, he is better off than most for sure. He owns a truck, enough said. But he has helped many, using his truck to take very sick people to the hospital in León, helping to start agricultural cooperatives, and sharing his own brand of Nicaraguan/Cuban hospitality with many. On Cully's walk to

Elio's home that fine morning, he counted more than twenty *guadarbarrancos*, the beautifully adorned national bird with an insanely long tail. For comparative purposes, that's like walking to the corner store and seeing 20 Bald Eagles chirping at you, in the span of 20 minutes; holy Moses that would be cool.

Everything is connected in Nicaragua. Take the story of water. In addition to the changes to the local climate, the copious, illegal use of water with impunity by a few local wealthy families, and the corrupt practices embedded in the local water committee, there is the problem of contamination. Insecticides and fertilizers that are spread on the local crops are just looking for somewhere to go when they have done their sterilization and killed off the pests. Naturally, they seek water. Some *pozos* (wells) are protected with an outer core that prevents groundwater from getting in, but the process to protect them is expensive, and most are not covered. Thus chemicals seep into the wells, people drink, get sick, and die, often from kidney disease, affecting it seems every family in El Tololar.

Contamination of water sources can also happen when the local public water system is down, and people need to haul water up from their natural wells. They often use a team of *bueys* (oxen), tie a rope to a bucket, and direct the bulls to walk away from the well, pulling the bucket up to the surface. During the process, the oxen poop on the rope, and the poop goes back into the water on the next haul. Feces and water shouldn't mix, and waterborne health problems persist.

When cute, fuzzy animals change their happy tune, it can be really quite scary. Take our frustrated rabbit Rainer. We have had Rainer for close to seven months, and all that time he has lived without a mate. For some time we thought he would get by as a loner, and as noted previously, he has tried his darndest to pretend our cat Mimi is a rabbit. Last week, however, Rainer's libido problems finally spilled over into violence, his full wrath being directed at Cully.

It started with a few, relatively innocent nips to the feet one morning, followed by a more aggressive feint at the legs several minutes later. Then, soon after breakfast, as Cully was walking into his room to feed the cat, he turned around to see a large white bunny, airborne and with teeth bared, literally flying at his left leg. In that split second, Rainer managed to both claw Cully's foot and make a good-sized bite into his leg. The action was so seemingly random that our first thought was that we had a rabid rabbit. Harlan and Olle quickly sequestered themselves in a bedroom, while Cully, now holding a broom handle, found himself stuck in the kitchen. Every time he tried to get out the bunny was there, jumping and biting at the broom. He finally crawled out the window with his broom, and walked into the field near the house. Don Leonel and Belkis heard the commotion. They came over and like everyone else since (except Cully) had no problems with the *conejo (*rabbit*),* petting and caressing him one minute as he charged Cully the next.

The bunny attack was certainly magnified in Cully's mind due to the fact that he had worked at a rabbit farm as a teenager- a farm that contained only big white bunnies with pink eyes (like Rainer) – and thus there was clearly some PTSD happening. In the end, the PTSD manifested itself in several ways. At different times throughout the following day, Cully could be found either sitting on top of our dining room table, cowering in a corner or once, jumping onto Miriam's body and almost knocking her over, nearly breaking his finger in the process. We are oscillating around our next move. Do we give Rainer away, so Cully doesn't have to live in constant fear of another rabbit mauling, or find an *embra* (female rabbit) so that Rainer can finally sow his oats.

Last Sunday, as we walked by Miriam and Carlos's house, we saw a mid-sized pig sprawled out on a table in their front yard, her neck slit. We naturally made some inquiries and found that this dead pig was the last of the brood of five that Miriam's pig Carmello had given birth to back in December. Miriam had since sold the other four, and was in the process of fattening this one up to sell at market, where at its current size she could have gotten about $55. But this little piggie will definitely not be going to market.

It turns out that the pig had gone for a morning walk – they are all largely free-range pigs here in the village – and never came home when Miriam rang the noon lunch bell. She went looking and found her, lying on the ground, strangled by her leash which had wrapped itself consecutively around and around a small tree and a banana plant in Adilsa's backyard, choking her to death. It was really sad but Miriam took it in stride. Then she, Carlos, Wilmar, and their cousin spent the rest of the afternoon getting the mini-sow ready to eat. This included pouring boiling water on her skin to loosen the bristly hairs prior to shaving off, cutting holes to string rope through her legs, hoisting her up a nearby mango tree, slicing her skin into sections for dried pork skin, and cutting her meat into portions for consumption. It was a long, pretty gross process. But that's how you dress down a pig, and later that night, we had more pork for dinner.

Harlan recently joined the "I got stung by a scorpion club", making him the fourth and final *Familia Lundgren* entrant into the exclusive group. He had just got out of the shower, a rare soothing hot shower as we had just checked into a hotel on the beguiling island of Ometepe. He used the towel that hung nearby to dry, and then as he went to put it around his waist, got stung on the elbow. His response indicated something bigger and badder than a wasp or a spider. Sure enough, a dark spot on the flip side of the towel revealed a scorpion. Harlan's elbow swelled, he had trouble closing his hand, and had a bit of tingling on his tongue. His condition improved rapidly, but he remarked a few hours later that he officially no longer likes scorpions; neither do the rest of us.

Earlier this week, we had the chance to be a part of another computer give-away ceremony at the El Tololar Secondary School. This Tololamos project started in 2011 and has been an instrumental motivator for students and their families in El Tololar and surrounding communities. Each quarter, Tololamos gives out a computer to the top performing students in the school. Very few people have access to computers, and receiving a refurbished computer with all sorts of software is truly a gift. We were honored to participate, and watching one father of a computer recipient stand up to speak and then break down in tears said so much about his gratitude and the real value of the project. Harlan and Olle felt a little weird standing up in front of a courtyard full of students staring back at them, but the ceremony provided a real-life education to them about the value of computers as tools of education; it turns out they are not just for gaming, who knew?

Chapter 20:
Save it in the Cloud, Yes Miriam-Sensei, The Magic Hour

Mid/Late May

The island of Ometepe is a jewel in the middle of Lake Nicaragua, the largest lake in Central America. Ometepe means "two hills" in the local *Nahuatl* language (the indigenous population who once inhabited the island). It is comprised of two distinct sides connected by a rather thin strip of land about three-quarters of a mile wide in the middle. It is a giant land mass that takes four plus hours to circumnavigate by car, truck or microbus, and slightly more by motorcycle, many of which are rented by tourists and subsequently smashed, due to the uneven roads and poor driving skills. Each side of the island is adorned with its very own volcano, really not "hills" at all, Concepcion on the left as you look at it from the port city of San Jorge, and Maderas on the right. We were staying on the Maderas side, so decided that we had to hike that particular – now dormant – volcano. Concepcion, on the other hand, is definitely not dormant and continues to smoke, gurgle, and bellow vapors on a regular basis.

We had been told that getting to the top of either mountain was a serious task, and that although Maderas was shorter by about 230 meters (1,394 in total), it was not easy to summit. We've hiked our share of mountains and volcanoes as a family so weren't concerned and as we headed out through the gently rolling cow pastures with our guide Anuar, we figured we had it in the bag. Anuar's knowledge of the flora and fauna was impressive and there didn't seem to be a stone he didn't know about – including the one in the middle of a cow pasture that he said a giant boa lived underneath. He showed us petroglyphs (made 1,200 years ago by the *Nahuatl*) and told us that the bright blue chickens we saw on the fringes of farmers' fields had been so painted to avoid being attacked by eagles, who apparently found blue an unsavory flavor.

We came upon a family of Capuchin monkeys as we ascended. They are more aggressive than their larger monkey relatives the Howler, who we heard howling their eerie, haunting, yet beautiful bellow our whole way up. Evidently the Capuchin do not like people – or anyone invading their space – and one flustered male started throwing sticks at us to be sure we moved along. We saw tons of trees, including the giant *Guanacaste* (the national tree of Costa Rica) and the huge *Ceiba* (the Guatemalan national tree, and one of the star attractions in the movie *Avatar*). Who knew trees could act?

We passed *cafetals* (coffee plantations), one of which had been left to fend for itself when its owner died suddenly and thus was a bit worse for wear, many of the plants sporting frail, broken leaves – and came to a small river, which we found out was the principal water source for all the surrounding towns. From the river, the trail went sharply up to the right, but that's an understatement.

In the US, when we make trails on steep inclines, we generally employ the switch-back method, whereby the trail zigzags its way up, minimizing the incline one has to hike. Not so on Maderas; there they take a "most direct route approach," fashioning paths straight up the mountain, regardless of steepness. It was this trailblazing technique that made our hike difficult, as the next two miles up consisted of non-stop, hand-over-hand climbing on wet, slippery rocks, roots, and mud. We were stinky and sweaty in no time, and marveled at how Anuar could stop, smoke a cigarette, and then continue on past us at a rapid pace, as if energized by the fumes in his lungs.

We finally did reach the top, where we were gifted with a panoramic view of… clouds (Maderas houses one of the few cloud forests in Nicaragua). But Olle and Harlan (kudos fellas, you earned that hike) were transfixed by actually being in a forest of clouds, and could have cared less that on that day there were no spectacular views to be had. We opted for not taking the additional three hour add-on which involved hiking down into the crater lake that sits at the top of Maderas, and thus were able to descend to our hotel in a respectable time, completing the total hike in about eight hours, albeit "surfing" much of the way down due to the mix of slippery trails, steep ravines on either side, and sneakers with no soles.

Back home in Massachusetts, when a teacher is sick, a team of substitutes stand at attention, ready to take over duties for the day. They fully understand – as do the students – that they won't be taken very seriously, but are generally able to administer some semblance of schoolwork, hand out bathroom passes, and admonish the occasional spitball shooter for the better part of 45 minutes. Nicaragua doesn't have such a safety net, and when a teacher is sick, the kids are sent home for the day. This, plus hiatuses from school due to excessive dust (especially in El Tololar during the dry season), torrential downpours, lack of electricity, and any of a variety of lesser-known holidays and teacher training days, means that students aren't getting schooled as many days as they should.

Last Wednesday, Miriam walked Harlan and Olle to school while Cully spent the day in León, looking to obtain gainful employment for our return trip. They followed our usual route, passing several peanut fields, dodging cow, horse, and pig patties, and arrived at school 45 minutes later. Olle's 4th grade class was running amuck, and Miriam soon found out from the headmaster, Samir, that Olle's *profe* (teacher) was home sick. Samir suggested that Miriam could take over duties and at least play some games with the kids and in true Miriam fashion, she jumped – or danced – at the opportunity. They started outside with stretches and jumping jacks, then moved inside for English class. English went well enough, as students shouted out words *(palabras)* they knew and soon had formed several categories, which they turned into basic sentences. Ding ding, class dismissed.

At this point Miriam was informed by 25 students that it was time for PE. Thus they went back outside, held PE which included kickball, races, and tag, and then re-entered the classroom for a valiant attempt at a math lesson. Unfortunately, only about half the students actually made it back into class and despite her best efforts, ten minutes into an attempt to teach the relatively new "lattice" multiplication technique, the remaining students had vanished, several remarking on their way out that it was now time for recess. But big props to Miriam, 4th grade *Profe* in a Nicaraguan School, if only for a day.

Random thought for the day:

From a distance, it can be hard to distinguish whether you are looking at a chicken's head or butt, until they decide to raise either body part and continue pecking at insects.

The rainy season has started, bringing with it a resurgence of ants (the dreaded *hormigas)* into every patch of ground, floor, grass, or garbage. They have essentially encircled our house, as they had up through November, again building mini-cities, food depots, and possibly exercise gyms, as they are definitely fit and ready to bite. We do our best to keep up with the daily hordes that stream onto our patio – often in search of Harlan and Olle's snack remnants – but we end each day on the losing side. Yes, we have our little victories in some of the smaller skirmishes, like when Cully took down a large hill outside our shower with a frenetic blast of chemicals from our overworked spray bottle. But we've got no shot at winning the war; they reproduce like rabbits.

Speaking of rabbits, we finally came up with a solution for Rainer our white hare. Rainer's hatred of Cully grew so severe that the two could not be in the same space without Rainer attacking his lower extremities and Cully leaping, shrieking or running as if he'd just seen a ghost, or a mouse. After several calls, the local Purina food and pet supplier in León managed to get a shipment of white rabbits – why, oh why is it always the white ones with pink eyes? – and Cully stopped by one rainy afternoon to choose Rainer a mate. The trip from Managua to León must have put a good scare into them – that and being in a small, stinky cage surrounded by weird humans – and their collective shaking and twitching made it difficult to determine who would be the best fit. In the end, "being female" was our only real requirement.

The nice woman who helped Cully lifted the animal up to gendertruth (a new but useful word, no?) its identity, and promptly plopped her in a box, where Shaky proceeded to wet the carton and the floor around her. The employee made extra holes and loosely lined the box with plastic, all the while sneezing and likely wondering why with such allergies she had chosen to work so closely to animals. One-hundred and forty *cordobas* later, Cully was walking toward the bus. The ride home went smoothly enough, except for the fact that the downpour outside required that all the windows be closed, resulting in the always popular "sauna bus." Rainer, henceforth forever housed in a hutch at Miriam and Carlo's house, definitely became the happiest rabbit on the block upon meeting his new mate; it was clearly love at first sight. As a bonus, Rainer's evil glares and feints at Cully now somehow seemed less angry and intense.

Our chickens Malam and Pagi are growing quickly, continuing to spend their days clucking and pecking over an area that spans across our yard and spilling over into Adilsa's, Aquiles, and at times Esteban's patios. Up until recently, no one had definitively *gendertruthed* either Pagi or Malam, but there was a growing consensus that Malam might actually be a rooster. This reality was hard for us to swallow, as it produced visions of boisterous, ear-piercing cock-a doodles every morning at an uncomfortably close distance to our house. Were we ever relieved one night when Harlan, walking back from the latrine, asked why there was a broken egg laying directly underneath a roosting and clearly perplexed Malam.

Now that Malam is officially a hen, our new problem is finding where she has been laying her eggs, as three weeks later we only have the one cracked shell as proof. We have tried to create other comfortable roosting places, and Olle is in the process of designing an egg-catching hammock to place under her current perch. But our best guess for now is that she is laying eggs on the thatch roof of our patio, a place she flies awkwardly to most days in search of insects. As of yet, we've had no whiffs or wafts of rotten sulphur, but we're just waiting.

We've done a lot of things here in Nicaragua that we couldn't have anticipated before coming. Planting and cultivating yucca, attending "the Day of the Dead," pursuing a life-size replica of Jesus down the street, and eating dried pigs blood delicacies as a snack (okay this was once, only Cully, and he didn't like it!). But marriage counseling in Spanish was definitely not our list. Yet somehow, last Thursday night we found ourselves imparting post-nuptial advice while seated at the dinner table, eating *gallo pinto* (rice and beans). Clearly our credentials were lacking in several categories (fluency in native tongue and accreditation at the forefront) but in the end, the two and one half hour session seemed to prove fruitful.

Much of our counsel focused on some of the communication skills we have learned to employ and found useful over our 13 years of marriage. And while our conversation spanned multiple different angles and levels of their relationship, our advice could all be summed up with just two basic guidelines. First, when providing feedback to your partner, don't use the pronoun "you." This comes across as accusatory and it is better to start with "I feel like…" This was definitely a new concept for our squabbling couple, as was our second, seemingly more obvious piece of advice, to not wave, point your finger, and vociferously gesticulate in the other person's face while calling them names. They appeared to really appreciate most if not all of our suggestions, and we can only hope that our Spanish was sufficiently clear so as to help and not exacerbate their problems.

Many of our bus rides to and from León can be quite monotonous, although each one seems to hold some sort of interesting cultural, language, or weather-related incident. Last

Friday's bus ride back to El Tololar on the 4:30 p.m. Lisandro Santiago bus involved an interesting blending of several different chicken bus-related phenomena. First, by the time we pulled out of the León station, the bus was packed to the gills. This left Miriam and Cully, as often is the case, standing while Harlan and Olle sat squished between a variety of different body types and sizes.

Next, Harlan had been feeling pretty sick all day and a bouncy, sweaty, bus ride wasn't doing his stomach any favors. Opening his window helped at first, but as a legitimate monsoon downpour started we were forced to close it. Next, a small boy near the front began to cry as we turned down the dirt road to Tololar, and as he was passed among family members and to the next seat buddy, his screaming began to reach fever pitch. At one point during the commotion, Adiac – the buses' outspoken and jovial *cobrador* (money collector) yelled from the back, in between making change for someone's fare, "put him on a breast." This comment, as one would expect set off a variety of responses from other passengers, and it was only when the young boy and his flustered family disembarked that the bus quieted down. The rest of the ride was much more sedate, except for Harlan's continued tummy problems and the venerable river rushing down the middle of the road, transforming Lisandro into more of a ship captain than a bus conductor.

Francisoco Martinez, Cesario Juarez, Kevin Castillo, Mayerling Escato, Dariana Urbina: these five students and many others were recent recipients of some of the clothes donated by many of our friends and families. We collectively thank everyone very much.

You know those rare moments when you are engaging in some type of activity, and the stars somehow align, allowing you to go farther or longer or achieve more than you ever thought possible? Harlan had one of those days not long back, while running in our peanut field. He had set out to do a respectable six laps, which already would have bested his previous farthest run in his entire life, the five laps (miles) he had done the week before. He was feeling good and before he knew it, five turned to six and six to seven. It was early evening, and a soft, steady, warm rain began to fall, cleaning the air of dust and making for the ideal running conditions. Eight, nine, ten, Harlan was still running strong. In the end, he experienced a magical, almost transcendent moment, reaching 12 miles and more than doubling his longest run ever. It's cool, right? When we realize that we can so often achieve much, much, more than we ever thought possible. Way to go Harlan.

Olle recently invented an interesting game, made possible only by the abundant supply of flies occupying our house. The game requires two players (minimum) and two *matar moscas* (sticky sheets of paper that flies land and die on). There are several variations, but really all you need is one player in the kitchen, for example, and the other on the porch. Each watches their *matar mosca* and calls out the updated number of flies whenever one lands and gets stuck. The highest number of dead flies wins. On an extremely hot afternoon or dreary, rainy morning, it can be an excellent way to pass the time. Thus far, our kitchen is beating our patio, by a lot!

In the middle of a flurry of activity one recent Sunday – which included cleaning up from the previous nights' rain storm, teaching class to the boys, attending to Harlan and his upset stomach, and making popcorn for the nights showing of the movie *Sandlot* – Carlos and Miriam dropped by, carrying a small, black, plastic bag. They dropped the bags' contents onto the ground, which included not one but two coral snakes they had found (next to a pair of scorpions) in a pile of wood near their house. Coral snakes are considered the most venomous of any snake in Nicaragua and even these small ones, a foot long at best, could have ended any of our days. Living near so many potentially dangerous animals can be a bit unnerving, and we thank Carlos for making things even a little safer.

On June 3rd, we will be hosting a running race in El Tololar to support the work of Tololamos in the community. The special thing about this race is that originally we thought it was going to be really small, with only forty or so participants, as running, running events, and even exercise are definitely not a big part of the culture. But thanks to some awesome publicity by Tololamos staff and volunteers, and a groundswell of interest by the public, we already have 150 participants, more than a week and ½ before the race. We are pretty sure with families, spectators and others, we will have 300 attendees. It's a testament to the great work of Tololamos in the community in the areas of health, education, and the environment, and we are excited about the significant change that is happening here in El Tololar.

Chapter 21:
The Chicharrón Guy, Goose bumps, Run Forrest Run

Early/Mid-June

The pepper, tomato, onion, banana, potato ladies can be found throughout León, but they tend to concentrate on bus terminals. They seem perennially happy as they board increasingly crowded buses, selling plastic bags filled with 5 – 10 of each type of vegetable, each bag usually selling for 10-20 *cordobas* (we are currently at just shy of 30 *cordobas* to the dollar). We have our favorites, like the young mother we buy our bananas from most days we take the Lisandro Santiago bus home to El Tololar. At 10 *cords*, her bananas are priced right, and as long as we eat them within two days, they are quite tasty. Some days we forget, and buy our bananas elsewhere, and our vendor friend is always taken back and a bit miffed at us that we don't need yet another bag.

In addition to the staple vegetable/banana ladies, we've made other food-based friends during our travels both through León and in El Tololar. There are the fellas that sell us our fruits and other vegetables in the market that abuts the bus terminal. We mainly buy from this one guy, José, but inevitably interact with his neighbors as well in halting Spanish, generally about soccer. Harlan is often wearing some colorful soccer shirt, and the guys get a kick out of ribbing him about his favorite team or player. José and Miriam seem to have a sort of cuisine connection, as she spouts out what we need (*una bolsa de cebollas* (a bag of onions), *tres pepinos* (three cucumbers), *cinco zanahorias* (five carrots), *dos sandias* (two watermelon), *y un ayote* (one pumpkin) and he moves like lightning, filling our shopping bags in rapid succession with our provisions for the week.

Other food friends include the ice cream guy (we generally have had our fill of sweets by the time we encounter him on the late bus but from time to time splurge on a cone), the soda lady (she sells soda (*gaseosa*) until she can't any more, often unaware that the bus has left the station, forcing her to disembark and walk back with a bucket of empty bottles perched precariously on her head), and, for lack of a better word, the "sweet, unhealthy cake" lady. She is one of our favorites and although we have yet to buy even a smidge from her due what appears to be cakes made of pure sugar and fat (they are therefore probably delicious), we love watching her shuffle down the aisle, cracking jokes with a deadpan face that slowly turns to a mischievous grin.

Our all-time favorite is the *chicharrón* guy (he sells bags of peanuts and fried, dried pig's skin). We rarely buy the *chicharrón* but love fist-bumping and talking with him every time we meet him on the bus – he's got a son in Miami). He arrives in León every morning at about 5:00 a.m., works the buses and streets all day long, and takes a late evening bus to the nearby city of Chinendega, arriving home around 9:00 p.m.. He has three kids, and works seven days a week exclusively to support them. You can tell he's a selfless guy, he genuinely cares about other people, and if he lived in our town, we'd definitely have him over for dinner. Despite the transient nature of our relationship, we consider Jose Manuel to be our *buen amigo.*

Most of the t-shirts worn in Nicaragua seem to be donations from the USA. The majority are written in English, and they can be comical when worn by an unsuspecting Nicaraguan who likely doesn't grasp a particular slogan's significance. There was the skinny tricyclo (3-wheeled bike taxi) driver who haggled over a client's fair wearing a shirt that read, "Of course I'm right, I'm Italian!" Or the giant, neckless weightlifter who looked like he could squeeze you in two. Somehow his countenance just didn't seem quite as scary when wearing a bright pink, incredibly tight t-shirt inscribed with the *Finding Nemo* quote, "Just Keep Swimming."

Miriam and the boys came home last week to witness a gross yet impeccably-timed series of events. First, they walked into the kitchen to find a large, dead rat on the floor (like, this was big) and our cat Mimi meowing proudly nearby. Miriam grabbed it by the tail and began carrying it outside when Mimi ripped it out of her hand, took it behind the fridge, and began munching on its head. Once the skull was gone, Mimi dragged the dismembered body out, clearly even prouder than before. However, when she least expected it, Miriam snatched the body and again began carrying it outside. This time, right as she crossed our patio threshold to go outside, down came rolling off the roof the answer to our previous query about where our hen had been laying eggs, one dropping and cracking right in front of Miriam and the headless rat. The egg roll moment must have been some sort of prophetic sign, and we are continuing to try and divine its deeper meaning.

Moments in life can be so fleeting. We often see something happening and say to ourselves, "Oh, I'm too busy to experience that right now. I'll do it later." But guess what, there usually isn't a later; later can just be a synonym for never. Take the gorgeous, giant, white flower that bloomed one morning last week on the edge of Aquiles' yard, about twenty yards off the edge of our patio. The flower was part of some type of cactus, and it opened wide to greet the 5:30 a.m. sunrise. We breathed and gazed in its beauty, and then said we'd go over later for a closer look. But life happened, and by the time we thought of it again, it had wilted and withered away under the late-morning sun. Do it… whatever it is, NOW!

We've written on several occasions about the *guadarbarranco*, Nicaragua's national bird. They are stunningly beautiful, and at times it can be unreal that there are so many of them living right near our house. Many seem to congregate these days behind our home, in the trees that separate our yard from Adilsa's beans and Don Leonel's corn, and we recently found out why. While heaving our usual daily double bucket combo (one pee, one garbage) into our waste pit one morning, low and behold what should fly out of a hole in the side of the ditch but a *guadarbarranco.*

We had noticed a series of openings lining the hole's perimeter, and had thought they belonged to an iguana, or were perhaps the work of a dog digging for extra food. But true to their name, the "guarder of the banks" had in fact been watching over our garbage hole, because surely something needed to protect it from all those mangy dogs. Perhaps the most remarkable thing about our sanitation bird is the discrepancy between its beauty and its surroundings, like a diamond in the rough. Don't you just love when that happens? When something exquisite sprouts out of the most unlikely of places, astounding us while making us test our preconceived notions of how the world operates.

Carlos and Miriam came by bearing five eggs last week, the work of our hen Malam, who has also begun laying eggs in the brush pile in their front yard. Despite where they came from, they assured us the tiny eggs would be tasty – and they were! We got talking about what it was like a year ago, before we had arrived. What did they expect our family to be like? What were they most nervous about? It turns out a few things.

First, they were embarrassed. They knew we were a "wealthy" family from the US – we had paid them to build us a whole house for goodness sakes – and they felt we wouldn't understand the poverty they lived in. They wondered if we would even be able to stay for a whole year, as life is so different in El Tololar compared to Massachusetts. They told us about the last day before we arrived. They were all running around like crazy, cleaning the house, cutting the yard, and putting the final touches on our home. They didn't know us from Adam, but were willing to open up their lives to us, to take a chance on some strangers. More than nine months later, we have collectively learned so much about each other; outsiders have become friends, the "other" has become "one of us."

Update on Malam the Hen: After laying a few eggs at our house and then deciding Carlos and Miriam's dump was a better place for eggs, Malam has subsequently found a boyfriend, the big white, totally vain rooster who crows at all hours of the morning around our house and walks around thinking he's God's gift to poultry. Somehow, our sweet Malam has taken a liking to him and they can now be seen sauntering around the yard together. They truly are an odd couple, and their union has resulted in Malam exploring other sleeping accommodations and leaving poor Pagi to roost all by her lonesome.

Update #2: Turns out Malam had in fact been sleeping under a giant pile of brush that Carlos and Miriam had been piling up in preparation for a big burn. After they torched it last week (we made sure Malam wasn't fried) she lost her digs and has now taken to roosting once again on our patio. Pagi has a companion again.

Goose bumps are found, mostly on arms and sometimes on legs, all around the world. They have a universal nature about them, and they don't distinguish between sex, religion, culture, or ethnicity. Thus they are connective, binding, and relational. They tend to appear either during really frightening moments, or when some experience (listening, seeing, touching, feeling) or emotion is so visceral that it goes beyond the norm, touching a part of our soul that rarely gets touched. Last week we had a party at Adilsa's house to celebrate four birthdays (Miriam, Harlan, Belkis, and Mariella) and to honor all the mothers in our midst (May 30th is Mother's Day in Nicaragua). Before the party, we put on a song written by Tololamos Executive Director Tyler St. Claire (he's kind of a jack-of-all-trades). As soon as Tyler began to sing, giant goose bumps appeared on both Adilsa and Cully's arms. The bumps spoke for themselves, relaying in an instant so much about Tyler and his impact in the lives of others.

Miriam and Cully have wanted to run a half-marathon ever since hearing of the eleven and one half laps that Tyler and Wilmar had run a few years back in the peanut field. They knew they couldn't run it the day of the Tololamos race so decided to attempt the run prior to race day. They started at about 3:50 p.m., meeting friends Yader and Fernando after one lap, and continued running for 13 laps. It was a hot day (it kind of always is here) and after about lap five they were both feeling heat exhaustion. But the sun began to go down, it got a little cooler, and they pushed on. By the time they were done, they were completely spent. Yader, on the other hand, looked like he could go on forever and in fact did do a 14th lap just for kicks. It wasn't easy, but they did the half marathon. The cost? That day up through midnight, both Cully and Miriam felt pretty ill, experiencing regular bouts of vomiting and nausea while they watched an early summer lightning storm role in.

We attended a ceremony at the local Catholic Church in El Tololar last week. It was the one-year anniversary of the death of our good friend Beto's grandmother. We just missed meeting her before she passed, but we hear she was an amazing, caring, and powerful woman when she died at 100 (if you are that old in Nicaragua, you likely don't know exactly when you were born, but 100 seems like it was at least in the ballpark). We entered the church, already sweating, and were ushered up to the front row. There was a new priest up front, and he took the opportunity of seeing the family of gringos up front to begin peppering his homily with a variety of English words. It turned out to be much shorter than most of the other two to three hour affairs we have attended at the church, and before we knew it we were outside eating sweet cornbread and drinking sodas, the requisite prepared refreshments for all the parishioners.

Prior to exiting the sanctuary, we had the chance to hug two of the woman's daughters (both in their late 70s or early 80s). Both of the women we already knew in passing from riding the bus, but our attendance on this day clearly meant something special, and it felt good to support and connect in a meaningful way. That feels good to all of us, doesn't it? Encouraging others in a time of need, and getting to know strangers in a more profound way in the process.

Preparations leading up to the first annual Tololamos *Carrera* (Race) last went according to plan – mostly – and were not unlike planning for a typical 5k race in the in the USA.

First, three of us – really Cully and Miriam watching Yader – spent the morning before the race hacking weeds with a machete, raking leaves, and kicking cow pies off the race course. Then, we borrowed Yader's Grandpa's oxen and hauled fifty rental chairs from Marisella's *venta* to Don Leonel's patio. Later in the day, Miriam went to Ivania's to help make 200 enchiladas and 200 fruit juices, while Cully and the boys helped begin positioning the items needed for the big day close to the racecourse/peanut field. Harlan interrupted us once during the day to see if we had an extra baseball kicking around, noting that his buddies had resorted to using a sour yet surprisingly hard lemon as their ball. That night, we held a big final preparation meeting at our house to finalize any last minute details, ranging from how much toilet paper to place in the latrines to where to place the bathroom signs.

Race morning dawned without a hint of rain in the sky, and by 4:30 a.m. the whole peanut field was a hive of activity with Telica volcano smoking in the distance. Some volunteers were laying down chalk lines, others hauling water buckets, and still others carrying tables and chairs over barbed-wire fences to the rim of the peanut field. *La Doctora* and three other representatives showed up from the Health Center, as did a group of awesome Spanish and Nicaraguan Volunteers carrying drums, tambourines, and face-painting supplies.

Miriam had made an excellent sign directing people to either Don Leonel's or Wilmar's latrines when nature called. Unfortunately, not long after posting, a cow walked by and ate the sign, causing minor consternation on the part of runners with nervous bowels. In the end the first race for Tololamos went amazingly well, and in all we had close to 300 attendees. There were 100-meter dashes in the 5- 7-year-old and 8- 10-year-old age groups. Next there was a one-kilometer lap for the 11- 14-year-olds, followed by a 200-meter open dash. The main event was the 5k (give or take), a 5-lap race around the peanut field, won handily by our friend Marden who clocked in at about 6 minutes per mile. Miriam and Cully were spent from their previous thirteen lap event, but Harlan and Olle both entered the one-lap race and finished respectably. The race was the first ever in El Tololar, and really brought the community together around health, education, and the environment. And, thanks to many of our family and friends, we were able to raise almost $2,000 for the work of Tololamos in the community.

Chapter 22:
The Last Waltz, Adios For Now, Muchisimas Gracias

The rain's been coming down pretty hard as of late, falling at its pleasure at all hours of night and day. A few weeks back, an especially strong afternoon rainstorm rolled in as Cully was coming home on the 1:30ish Mariano bus. The road was a river, and as he disembarked, Miriam was there to meet him with a raincoat and a smile. She had fought her own torrent of water to get to the bus stop – ideally situated at the bottom of a hill frequented by every cow in El Tololar – and thus had been standing in a feces flow for the better part of fifteen minutes. They hiked in shin-high water up the hill and made it to the house with a mostly-dry computer and minimally soggy groceries.

The storm roared on all afternoon, and the first half hour after arriving home was set aside for sweeping water off the patio, shifting Olle's bed out from under a leaky roof, and monitoring the multiple trickles springing from Miriam and Cully's ceiling. The electricity flickered but stood fast, yet ironically the water shut off. The clothes drying on the line had got soaked for the third day in a row, the flies were seemingly everywhere, and it had been another rough day of schooling on the home front. It was a seminal moment; was it time to get annoyed and frustrated at the general dreariness of the situation? Alternatively, should we just laugh in the face of aggravation? In the end a third option was decided on, one that included popcorn, cloistering in a room, singing a few songs, and having a frank conversation about the challenges and lessons of living in Nicaragua for a year.

We often take things for granted when they are a part of our everyday life. These things become almost like background noise – maybe it's your neighbor starting her or his car every morning, or the mini-mart cashier you say hi to on your evening commute. We don't pay much attention to them, but they are comforting in their commonness, their normalness. They make us feel safe because they are always there, present but not intrusive.

Here in Nicaragua, there are plenty of things we will miss; somewe've taken for granted, while others we've just gotten so accustomed to being around. We'll miss (some of us will) the chirping sounds of myriad lizards in the beams above our beds, every chirp a sign that we can sleep knowing that lizzy will eat the night bugs. We'll miss the majestic views of smoking volcanoes (Telica, San Cristobal) all around us, and the cows, horses, and trees that serve as living, munching, growing images, framing the landscape. We'll miss the children in their white and blue school uniforms, walking to and from school down dusty or muddy roads or across wide pig-inhabited, green peanut fields. We'll miss the sound of Carlos or Aquiles sharpening their machetes the night before a big chopping, slicing or cutting job. We might even miss the "thunk, thunk, thunk" sound you hear on the chicken bus, produced by an errant branch whacking each window frame as it quickly approaches and then smacks you, squeezed up against the side because of the large woman's behind taking up three-quarters of a seat meant for no more than three 7-year-olds.

It'll be hard not to be able to fist bump the bus terminal attendant who goes out of his way to connect with us as we board the bus to El Tololar, or the smiling old man with glasses who sells us our *La Prensa* newspaper at the far-end of the terminal. Oscar, the gentleman who runs our favorite *venta* will be missed; he always smiles and comments about how excellent Harlan and Olle's Spanish has become. It will be hard to find a place in Boston to buy enchiladas as good as Alma's little *comedor,* which doesn't look like much but tastes like fried heaven after a long, dusty bus ride.

We'll miss the impromptu stop-bys at our house throughout the week by any number of friends:Beto, Adilsa, Yader, Fernando, (usually with his most recent work of art) Marden, Miriam, Carlos, Chico, Don Leonel, Yessica, Denis, the baseball boys, Belkes, Franklin, Maynor. Miriam will miss her special times cooking with our friend Ivania, and the extraordinary time we've had just to be together as a family. We'll miss the people the most--their tstories, smiles, and openness to others.

None of us will miss the flies, gnats, mosquitoes, biting ants, mangy, barking dogs, water shortages, or the incessant dust and dryness in the winter followed by equally incessant rain and summer mud. We won't miss the 2-4 a.m. rooster cacophony, followed by the 5-7 a.m. rooster cacophony (well we might, in a "that was a once-in-a-lifetime kind of experience" sort of way). We likely won't miss our pee bucket, or having to use a latrine for number two for a year, or only having cold, usually dark, dank outdoor showers. "Missing" might not be the correct word for how we'll feel about not having to dodge or smell roadside cow diarrhea after a storm – what do these bovine eat anyways? More fiber, *por favor.* We just won't feel too much nostalgia over no longer having to wipe white mold off the handle of our kitchen knife after only a two-day absence or needing to scrub pink/green mold off our room doors after one too many days of unshakeable humidity.

We had always been told that before peanuts *(mani)* came to town, the only previous destructive crop that had frequented these parts was cotton. Both *mani* and cotton (*algodon*) have their own stories which you can read more about in previous chapters. *Tempate* trees represented another foreign effort (this one by Austria) to cultivate, grow and harvest a non-native, questionably beneficial product. This was in the early 1990s, and it seems that the *tempate* strategy (as is often the case with many well-intentioned but misguided non-indigenous money-making schemes) started off strong. *Tempate* definitely gets the environmentally- friendly nod over both cotton and peanuts, planted as it was with the goal of producing biofuel from its seeds. An added , perhaps unexpected advantage of the *tempate* seed – as relayed by locals – is that if you mix the juice from seven seeds in one liter of water, it is very useful as a remedy for both kidney problems and incontinence.

Tempate may have ultimately had very positive environmental and economic returns but for a pesky worm. This omni-present little guy began devouring the tree's seeds by year three. A noble attempt was hastily made to plant another tree – called *Nin* – next to the *Tempate. Nin* has naturally occurring anti-worm repellent properties and seemed just the tree for the job. But N*in*, too, promptly succumbed to a different insect plague, leaving both the Austrian investors (and the Nicaraguan farmers they had given hope to) with nothing but a novel, slightly acidic, pee-suppressing juice – made from the few trees that remained – as their profit.

A few good lessons can be gleaned from the Nicaraguan experience of all three non-indigenous crops that have been part of the El Tololar story: peanuts, cotton, and *tempate*. First, do your homework on the front end. Only with community buy-in will a project be successful. Second, use the knowledge of locals. They have been farming the land for centuries, and therefore have a unique understanding of the land, climate, and culture. This can make them valuable allies, not adversaries. Lastly, ensure that the entire local community (people, land, resources) benefit, and are not deprived, as a result of the project.

How does a typical weekend day unfold for our family in El Tololar? Here's one recent take. It started with roosters – of course – and then an extended stretching time for Miriam and Cully, both of whose bodies have required regular exercise to combat their painful bed and soccer-induced cramps and sores. During exercises, Mimi the cat could be seen along the fence-line playing with an injured bird. Not five minutes later, the bird – now dead – was behind our stove being batted around by Dark Paw, the kitten we had gifted to Don Leonel four days earlier. Dark Paw, along with our other kitten, Dusty, – so named for her obsession for sleeping in our dustbin – both resisted living elsewhere and returned long enough to pee in the kitchen corner and ravage the poor dove.

After Cully had managed to scoop the mangled bird out of the kitchen, feathers flying everywhere, a sizeable scorpion appeared on the kitchen wall, not far from where Miriam was bleaching our mold and spider-ridden suitcases as we prepared for our return home. We killed him, just as Olle returned from playing with Rachel, our five-year-old neighbor who he patiently plays with on many occasions. Rachel had apparently informed Olle that she no longer wanted to play, following his disclosure that her kitten Figaro – whom she was supposedly looking for- had in fact died more than five months ago.

The rest of the morning's events included Cully stepping on a giant ant hill as he tossed the pee bucket contents not far from where Gray, our neighbor's puppy, was sipping water out of the kitchen sink outflow pipe, milk-flavored this day as Cully had inadvertently tossed sour milk down the sink rather than in the backyard garbage hole. Gray had a bad looking gash on her side, likely from either a dog fight or from being launched into the air by a cackling Rachel. Later that day, in the same milk canal, one could find Miriam and Carlo's pigs wallowing, an activity that has resulted in the side of the house (including the nearby shower) smelling increasingly like a genuine sty.

Here in El Tololar, it's easy to forget that being connected to everything through the internet is the norm back home. It's definitely not here. There is no Internet at our house or anywhere nearby, so we have grown accustomed to living without being wired. We no longer check our phones every five minutes for that telltale buzzing sound that foretells an incoming email. It's really cool to be unlinked, even if only for a year. And yet, it's also hard not to be able to connect with family and friends on a regular basis. So we try our best to hold the two in tension.

Before we arrived ten months ago, there were a lot of things to be scared or worried about, and even now as we leave, we feel that God has often had our back. Living with children in an environment with minimal access to healthcare is not easy, and something parents here just have to deal with. A day has not gone by in Nicaragua where Miriam and Cully have not thought – with some apprehension – "where the heck are Harlan and Olle and are they all right?" Besides the scorpions, tarantulas, snakes, and disease-infested fly presence, we have succumbed to many undiagnosed rashes, ailments, and peculiar disorders. Then there are the stories of dangerous encounters that we hear about, or see etched on others people's mugs. Both Larry and Alicia, for example, have scars on their faces from running full speed into barbed-wire fences, Larry's having barely missed scraping his eye out. Harlan and Olle cross and run near barbed-wire fences every day… and jump out of trees, play near rusty nails and broken glass, and… thank God they are safe!

There came a point, about a month and a half ago, when collectively we kind of hit our local food threshold. It started with a stab at eating less beans, brought on by a rather rapid and unexpected increase in daily, *frijole*-induced flatulence. Even the sight of beans began to make us nauseous at times, and soon rice, *plàtano* (plantain) chips, and various sweet drinks began to join the food strike. It came in waves, and we have eaten beans and many local foods since, but *legume-itis* is apparently a thing. We'll definitely miss the Nicaraguan food after we leave, but we won't mind having a few burgers and a pizza pie or two in between.

Conversations about mosquitoes and the diseases they carry – while you are actually in the process of getting stung by mosquitoes – can be unnerving. We recently had a final conversation with our 97-year-old friend Maria Jerez. As we conversed with Maria – on a patio surrounded by mud, standing water, and other excellent larvae breeding grounds – she kept shifting in her chair, complaining about the severe pain she had in her joints from a bout three years back with chikungunya, an extremely dangerous mosquito-borne illness that produces awful symptoms akin to or worse than its more famous disease cousins, malaria and dengue. As Maria talked, we couldn't help but imagine what poison our legs and arms were being injected with. We've had similar conversations with

Denis and Aquiles. Both of them contracted chikungunya about the same time as Maria, and now suffer from severe joint pain (Denis) and an inability to move his right arm at night in bed (Aquiles).

At times, we have conversations about what we have actually accomplished since we arrived last September 1st in El Tololar. It can be hard to quantify results when you haven't had a specific job title or description. Yet this predicament has forced us to look deeper into our daily lives, exploring and mining for the experiences and moments that have made a difference for others, and for us. So following a post-dinner family meeting under our rancho not long ago, we came up with the following catalog of accomplishments. Each and every one of them has been made possible because of the Tololamos team, the great people of El Tololar, and loved ones' unwavering financial and emotional support. THANK YOU!

We built a house:

Actually, Aquiles, Nestor and Carlo did, but many people helped provide the funds for the house – about $6,000. The house – a darned pretty one we might add – will soon be passed onto our friend Miriam. Her family will live there, an asset they would never have been able to afford on their own.

A horse:

For about $160 (the price of a room for one night in a not very nice NYC hotel) we bought a horse for Ivania after her previous horse died. The new horse has enabled her to continue bringing food to the school to sell to students each day, providing an invaluable source of income to her family.

A plan:

We assisted Wilmar in developing the first business plan for his computer business.

A business:

We provided $500 as an initial start-up investment in Wilmar's computer business. That investment, along with other support and a lot of sweat equity on his part, enabled Wilmar to launch his computer business (repairs and sales) in León. Wilmar's ultimate goal is to make enough money to be able to bring his wife Mariella (currently working sixteen hour days in Managua) to El Tololar. They want to live together with their daughter Rachel as a family. Wilmar's business is still a work in progress. He had to shift locations and focus more on selling and teaching software classes than repairing. But we are rooting for him, big-time.

Another Business:

We invested $200 in training and capacity-building for our friend Belkis, who also wanted to start a business in León so that she can actually live together with her son Leo. She's now self-employed as a massage therapist, and things are looking up!

Scholarships:

We are sustaining five high school students and two university students with scholarships. For just over $2,000 a year, these students (all promising scholars in tough economic circumstances) receive a monthly stipend for transportation, food, and books that allows them to stay in school or pursue their career dreams at the university level.

Micro-Investments:

We gave small Christmas gifts of money to a few local families. They weren't much ($50 bucks each) but in one case, that small investment made the difference between having to quit their small business – and being able to continue on.

Guide Training:

Our friend Yader – in training to be a tourist guide – needs practice, especially with foreigners so he can practice his English. We hired Yader (paying out about $150 total) to be our guide on several hiking excursions (including the deliciously fun but grueling hike we did up Volcano Telica in early April).

Cash-For-Work:

Instead of chopping our hands (or heads) off with a machete, we hired Carlos – and sometimes Larry and Aquiles – to cut our lawn and do other jobs around the house. They are much better at it then us, and besides, they needed the cash. So we invested in them (about $200 bucks total), and by extension helped support the local economy. By comparison, the average annual salary in Nicaragua is about $1,200.

Cash-For-Life:

There are a group of very smart people who have spent years researching the best ways to help people who are in tough economic circumstances. Their results are far from definitive, but they have come to the conclusion that simply giving people cash is the best way to help them. Why? Because people know their needs, and those living on the edge generally spend money on the things they need the most. These researchers feel that we could save a lot of money – and bureaucracy – by giving money, instead of implementing complicated programs laden with lots of red tape. Our family feels that smart NGOs like Tololamos and others actually do a great job of identifying problems and dispersing funds in an equitable way with minimal overhead. But just to test out these researchers theory, we made multiple, discrete cash outlays to various families – totaling about $800 – with no strings attached. These people were extremely grateful, and we feel confident the money is going to necessities much more than desires.

Bed-For-Work:

We hired Yader's Dad Yader to make us a bed, hoping it would be a vast improvement on our first bed, dubbed by some "the world's most uncomfortable bed." It never quite lived up to the hype from a comfort standpoint, but at $100 it is beautiful, and provided Yader with much needed income to support his family and bed-making business. The bed, we can rest assured, is now being slept on by Carlos and Miriam.

Bike Dreams:

We provided Miriam and Carlos with $300 as a down payment on a motorcycle. It's hard to say just how impactful a motorcycle can be for someone, but it can really make a huge difference. Just think about how hard it is to get by where you live without a mode of transportation. Then add that thought to the following equation: dirt roads + minimal public transportation + long distance to school multiplied by very few resources = I could really use a bike. So a bike is huge…

Helping Health:

Donations and material aid resulted in over $1,500 to support the local health clinic. This included basic amenities like chairs for waiting patients and electric fans, to a variety of medical supplies including antibiotics, bandages, glucometers and much more. For an insufficiently stocked local health outpost serving thousands of people each year, these contributions have been immensely valuable.

Clothes Encounters:

Many friends and family donated clothes, valued at close to $1,000. T-shirts, shoes, sneakers, pants, hats, sweatshirts, dress-shirts, and socks to local families were provided to scholarship recipients, and students at Rebekah Rivas Elementary School. A well-made piece of clothing goes a long way here – clothes take a beating so strong fabric is highly prized – and these donations won't wear out anytime soon.

Barking up the Right Tree:

Donations from Harlan and Olle's school back in Massachusetts – Go Tucker Elementary! – toward the nursery (*vivero*) project led to $702 dollars raised through an old-fashioned coin drive. That is enough money to buy 10,000 seeds, 6,000 to 8,000 bags, hire workers to fill the bags, improve the irrigation system, pay for someone to watch and care for the saplings, publicize the project, and offer tree varietals and planting advice to anyone in the community who wants it. Wow!

Does Compute:

Many in our network (including good old Tucker School parents and families) donated over twenty devices, valued at over $1,000, (laptops, smartphones and tablets) to be used by Tololamos in a variety of ways, including as gifts to high-performing students in local schools.

Play Ball:

Between donations of soccer balls and baseball equipment (gloves, balls, hats) you helped provide over $500 worth of sports gear to a previously, very austerely outfitted baseball team and to several local elementary school gym classes.

The Human Race:

We helped put on the first ever race in El Tololar to support the education, health and environmental work of Tololamos. In all, we raised about $2,000 and initiated what we hope will be an annual event fostering a more intentional community mindset about the importance of health, the natural world, and exercise.

In addition to the financial and material backing, other people's support of Familia Lundgren over the past year also allowed us to take part in so many great activities in the community. Here is a snapshot, in rhyme:

> We helped plant yucca, in Nestor's field nearby
>
> Sowing seeds, cultivating, and dodging cow pies
>
> The corn harvest happens, once every year
>
> And so in January, we cut maize from ear to ear
>
> We served as judges in a battle of some singers
>
> These students were real artists and man there were some ringers
>
> We taught English class, twice a week for a while
>
> Some students learned a little, while others learned a pile

We helped Adilsa at the library, learning Dewey Decimal

It may be kind of passé, but that system is no bull

We had a big Thanksgiving Dinner, as a way to thank our peeps

Miriam cooked a giant batch of pasta, people seemed to like it heaps

We instigated soccer games, every Sunday afternoon

They became a huge event, from September until June

Twice a month we showed a flick, different films every time

Everyone was welcome, and it didn't cost a dime

Most of all this year, we learned anew to love our neighbors

That we may be different on the outside, but our souls are just like theirs

The Year in Summary

by Harlan Ray Keith Lundgren

This year has been an amazing mix of fun, sadness, hardship and learning. I think in the end I will come away with a good experience. In the end, I have seen rewards, such as after hundreds of times going out to practice baseball with the group of boys, and after enduring months of teasing, the last Saturday here I made the Tololar baseball team. We beat a neighboring community, Los Positos, in a big two games. I have seen many rewards but am super excited to see the end. It has been a good, hard year.

The Year in Summary

by Olle Winslow Lundgren

In Nicaragua, I have felt a lot and learned a lot. One of the things was I learned how to respect other people and to respect the culture. I have felt sad, happy, and missing the USA. This year has been hard.

Poem

by Miriam

To feel understanding

Real

understanding

You must stand, for a long time

in the shoes of another person's life

It can be a tug,

a drudge

pulling us out of all sense of comforts

zones and placements

OH but to understand to really Understand

IS A GIFT.

So what do you say on the other side of everything? When you are looking backwards at hundreds of experiences and emotions, ready to return from whence you came? How can you encapsulate, in a paragraph, just how deeply, and painfully, and graciously, and thankfully you have felt during the past year? It can't be done justly, so perhaps simply noting the few key words that have been our allies and friends this year will suffice.

We've learned what it means to have *grace* for ourselves and others. We've experienced a deep connection with the *other*. We've come to understand on a deeper level the power of *community* – a community that includes our new friends here and our friends and family back home. We've had the opportunity to take a big *risk*, and are now reaping the rewards in so many ways. We've seen *faith* in action, and we've felt *acceptance*. We've had a chance to live a *dream*, in the midst of all its messiness, pain, and complexity. We've witnessed the *kindness of strangers*, and seen strangers change into friends.

Today, we finalize this last chapter from the Camino Real Hotel in Managua, the same hotel our first chapter came from, exactly ten months ago.

Last night, a farewell party was held on our behalf on Don Leonel's dusty patio/soccer pitch. Sixty of our closest friends from the past year showed up, and we danced way into the night. There were some beautiful comments made by lots of people – including Harlan and Olle, in Spanish – and lots of tears shed. It was like we were trying to suck the marrow out of each moment, knowing that our time – for now – was up.

This morning we woke up at 5:15 a.m. and over the course of the next hour, people started arriving, appearing from across fence lines, behind trees or out of the blue. We were all tired, but every family member and friend showed up to say one final goodbye. They brought a *carretón* (horse-drawn carriage) and we piled our eleven bags on top. All the kids pushed and pulled the cart down the dusty road to the bus stop. Twenty minutes and many tears later, we boarded the Mariano bus to León for the last time.

Tomorrow, we leave a life we've loved, at times loathed and learned so much from. We leave Nicaragua, for now. Our goal is to return every year, continuing to build relationships with our new family and friends here. In addition, we have been asked to join the Board of Directors of Tololamos. Thus, we are excited about investing our time, money and souls into this truly special little part of the world.

From the bottom of our hearts, we thank you ALL for being with us on this journey, every step of the way.

Enjoy this day, your family, your friends… and your strangers. Learn from the people you don't know, seek out those who are different, and search for community in even the most unlikely of places… it's there!

Que te vaya bien

Cully, Miriam, Harlan and Olle

Epilogue

The book was written during rainstorms, with dust devils playing nearby, in hammocks, with chickens and seemingly rabid rabbits biting toes, under termite-laden ceiling beams, as seasons flowed by, and in between conversations with neighbors, with the baseball boys around, on concrete floors, sweating; a compilation of many small, seemingly fragmented pieces that make up a bigger story. In many ways it was written as our lives often unfold. Seconds, minutes, hours, days—they all flow together and in the midst of their passing we try to cobble together a coherent picture of who we are and who we want to become. We often think we fail, but it is in the midst of our daily blunders and monthly mishaps that we manage to construct messy but beautiful, serpentine lives.

We arrived back in the US in early July 2017 and it wasn't long before we were on another cross-country road trip, heading east back to Milton, MA and the life we left behind. In Yellowstone and the Grand Tetons we found ourselves driving past majestic mountains and equally amazing wildlife. Like our road trip prior to leaving for Nicaragua, we were awestruck by the sheer size, diversity and raw beauty of this country. And, as culture shock began to set in, we were at times taken aback by the affluence and easy access to material "things" that now surrounded us. But we were extremely happy to be back, and to be together as a family on the flip side.

While we each experienced re-entry differently, in those first few weeks we all sometimes felt that we were outsiders, interlopers watching ourselves engage and operate in a foreign world. We had often felt the same way in Nicaragua, and now perhaps this consciousness gave us a better ability to stand in the shoes of anyone who has been made to feel like an alien in our land.

We spent the last night of our road trip at a monastery in Maine, the same monastery where we started our journey, almost exactly one year before to the day. As we watched the sunset over the harbor, for the last time before our impending final return home, emotions flowed freely; we laughed, cried, and soaked the marrow out of that last moment of living this crazy, year-long odyssey. Together, somehow, Team Lundgren had done it. Or were we now just beginning?

The epilogue to this book was started almost a year ago. So much has changed for the Lundgrens and the world since then. And every time I (Cully) sit down to write, something else changes in the world, or our lives, or in Nicaragua, that makes me want to take a pause. I find myself wanting to wait until the world stops for a moment. Then, at least, I would have a brief instant where I could write really fast and get everything down on paper. And be done.

But life is ALWAYS changing, and nothing stays the same. We have to find a way to operate in that tension.

We left Nicaragua almost a year and a half ago. We left a country that was still the second poorest in the western hemisphere – after Haiti – but at least seemed to be exhibiting some encouraging signs of economic progress. The tourism industry was beginning to grow, English schools were popping up, and jobs in the city seemed to be more plentiful. But hiding underneath the shine of some encouraging signs was the reality that a very corrupt government was still in control, and that most Nicaraguans were living in poverty.

In April of 2018, protests against the policies and practices of the Ortega Government erupted across Nicaragua. Ortega had announced he was making cuts to social security benefits while increasing worker contributions at the same time. In a country where people have seen the opulent lifestyles of Ortega's family and friends, you can imagine this didn't go over so well. The protests erupted literally the same day that Larry, our friend from El Tololar, was returning to Nicaragua after having spent three months living with us and attending an English School in Boston. As this epilogue is being penned in October 2018, hundreds of Nicaraguans have been killed in nationwide protests and the economy has come to a grinding halt. Elsewhere in Latin America, a massive caravan of people looking to escape violence and poverty and seeking a better life have entered Mexico and are heading for the US border as I write. Trump is calling troops to the border. I shudder at what this all means, and wonder if we can unite somehow, some way.

GDP and national poverty statistics, numbers, never tell the real story, and we have witnessed the impact of the current climate in Nicaragua through the lives of our friends in El Tololar.

Our good friend Belkis had opened up a small *venta* (store) late last year, selling food and basic supplies out of her home. When the protests started, though, people stopped shopping, partly because transportation was disrupted but also because work had dried up. Marden, one of the rising young tour guides in León, was laid off from the tour company he worked for and was trying to look for work elsewhere, possibly in Costa Rica. One of the college students we have been supporting with a scholarship had to drop out of school.

Nestor had lost his job with one of the local phone companies, and was being chased down by loan sharks. He had needed money to plant yucca as an additional income source for the family and had taken out and exorbitantly high interest loan – his only option – the year earlier. Because of the economic collapse brought on by the protests and particularly bad weather, Nestor now needed a miracle ($6,500 to pay off the loan) or he could end up in jail. His family tried to sell a portion of the land they owned, but so far there have been no takers.

I hope a new, promising government is elected soon. I hope jobs come back. I hope all Nicaraguans get access to the same kind of opportunities we have here. We hope that in Nicaragua and across the globe, we can all find ways to work together, to achieve some sort of confluence, multiple rivers of backgrounds, ideas, and beliefs flowing together toward a better more equitable world, in the midst of all our differences.

Miriam and I will continue to serve as board members of Tololamos. Harlan and Olle will continue to see the world through a different, more understanding lens because of Nicaragua. Our family will always stay connected to the families who took us in, who shared the best kindness of strangers with us from day one, and taught us a new, more generous way to love. And we will always be grateful to all our friends and families who took a chance on supporting our Nicaraguan adventure, one we will never forget. Thanks for entering in with us. Stay in touch.

Cully, Miriam, Harlan, and Olle

Made in the USA
Middletown, DE
13 December 2018